It is essential to linger frequently
on the frontier of one's limitations,
looking out eagerly...

Across the Unknown

Books on Spiritual Growth by Stewart Edward White:

The Betty Book

Across the Unknown

The Unobstructed Universe

The Job of Living

The Road I Know

ACROSS
THE UNKNOWN

by Stewart Edward White
& Harwood White

ARIEL PRESS
Columbus, Ohio

First published by E.P. Dutton & Co. 1939
First Ariel Press edition 1987

This book is made possible by a gift
to the Publications Fund of Light
by James & Lois Blumenstiel

ACROSS THE UNKNOWN

ISBN 0-89804-150-3

TABLE OF CONTENTS

PART I—EXPLORATION

PART II—DEVELOPMENT

PART III—USE

AUTHOR'S NOTE

The present volume, like its predecessor *The Betty Book*, is a matter of collaboration in which so many people have been involved that it is difficult to name an author for its title page. There were, of course, those who gave us the material on which it is based— the Invisibles; anonymous and probably numerous. There was Betty who transmitted it. There was I, who took it down and typed it and filed it in loose-leaf books. And finally there was my brother, Harwood, to join us in selecting and arranging and digesting and presenting it in a form acceptable and valuable to others outside our small group. No trifling job, this last, for by the time we got at it, we had over two thousand single-spaced pages out of which to quarry about three hundred double spaced pages of text. It is for the form, then, that we on the title pages assume responsibility.

For the sake of clarity it should be mentioned that whenever the pronoun of the first person comes into the narrative, it refers to myself. The reason for this is that it seemed wise, to all of us, to illustrate occasionally by actual individual experience.

Stewart Edward White

The acts of your days on days make a certain-shaped thing of you. Then in the rhythm of life the influences too big for control strike a sharp blow or stroke or influence or vibration of some kind, that overcomes your own plan or sense of direction. And this same stroke arranges your relationships quite automatically. Suddenly you fit into the place where the thing you shaped will go with mathematical nicety. It is as though a lot of scattered things were dancing about; and clap! they were all in a pattern. You call it fate, or luck, or destiny, but all the time it is just the preparation of your days on days, your own deliberate handiwork. It is as though we were all put through graded sieves that suddenly reveal our sizes to ourselves; where usually we are all so mixed together that you could not measure. No amount of jiggling could shake you into a place you did not fit, for which you had not shaped yourself. Only when you are too inert to shape yourself are you at the mercy of the Pattern Maker.

ACROSS THE UNKNOWN

PART ONE

EXPLORATION

The struggle of each generation is the interpretation of the whispered allotment of wisdom into the current vernacular. You are at the turning of a great tide. Who is there to offer guidance in the age-proven technique of living, and yet point ahead to the regions we are appointed to explore? We arraign your generation for its failure to establish faith in the proven laws of living. Will you not voice it in this book of yours? Let honest conviction ring out; and strike a new note of responsibility.

What an awful region of words I've come to! I don't like them; they're just empty clamshells standing for things that aren't there!

I am greatly handicapped by my seeing the subject. Seeing the subject makes it too big for the words, and they stumble.

CHAPTER I

OUTFITTING

We are here recommending to you a country beyond. We think you will find its exploration rewarding. But we shall not be able to go along. We must merely tell you about it; and thus, perhaps, help you to find your own way.

This country is not something brand-new that we have been the first to discover. Others have passed this way before us. But they have been too few. The topography is not yet well understood, nor is travel there secure. Safe, well-made trails do not exist—only ways-through along which predecessors have here and there erected markers. And these routes are only for the sure-footed, for they are slippery and dangerous. Their exploration is not a tour, but an adventure.

This is a fact. But I think we are often told so in the wrong way. Mostly we are warned off. Stay out, is the cry, for this is a land of bugaboos! Some of the warnings, especially in symbolism, are terrifying. And, to my mind, somewhat misleading. Astral entities, dugpas, incubi and succubi, obsessing diabolisms, black magics of all sorts—if we listen to the East; queerness, crankiness, separateness, illusion, split personality, all the mental aberrations right up to actual insanity—if

3

we listen to the West: there are the perils which we must undertake if we are to dare in venturing. Pause and consider, they tell us solemnly; you need not venture, but if you do, make up your mind to face these enemies and dangers.

The dangers are real enough, I believe, in whatever terms they are stated. But they should not be terrifying, and certainly not deterring.

Did you ever read a pilot book of the Pacific Northwest Coast? It was written by a pessimist. His favorite phrase is "should not be attempted without local knowledge." Scattered through his pages are gems of description telling of the masses of ice "grinding together in tide whirls of great velocity." A winter fireside perusal could easily convince a suggestible man that only a miracle could keep him from disaster. And the author tells the truth. These perils of sunken ledge and treacherous current, compelling tide whirl, clashing ice, are all there. But to a man with ordinary foresight and common sense they are slight menace—provided he meets them well-informed and well-prepared.

Just so, I conceive, these great and very real dangers to irresponsibles, in this country beyond, are not of the sort among which one must walk in dread—provided he is suitably equipped for the journey. Was it Stefansson who defined the usual "adventure" as merely a lack of preparation. That is what I am trying to emphasize here: the importance of a little careful preparation.

Before proceeding further, we must first of all agree on the matter of words. Unfortunately some of the words we must use are pretty well tattered by careless use. They have frayed out into numerous rags of connotation. They have been spread thin to cover too many aspects, each of which really should have a word of its

4

own. If we could find, or make, fresh words, we should get on much better. But there are none; and the results of our fabrication are both clumsy and cold. So we must do our best in freshening, defining, limiting.

First, we must retread the term "psychic." That has become a very skiddy word; but it is the only one we have. For this adventure into another region of consciousness is psychic; and it uses psychic faculties. Only, unfortunately, the term covers too many things. With some of them we have no concern at all. Some of them we utilize as a means to the end we are after. All of them are more or less disputed territory.

Broadly speaking, they present two aspects. Into one general classification we may crowd that great mass of astonishing and debated phenomena: ectoplasm and all its varied manifestation, clairvoyance, telepathy, direct voice, apport, spiritism, clairaudience, levitation, and such. By most of us these have always been regarded with suspicion or downright disbelief. Nevertheless, such a weight of evidence has accumulated that they can no longer be dismissed by a mere scornful wave of the skeptical hand.

In the second aspect we include a number of things of perhaps more general toleration. Nevertheless, the average man still lumps them as at least queer or impractical: concentration, meditation, prayer, communion, Yogi exercises, cosmic consciousness—even intuition, inspiration and genius. The names associated with many of these are unfortunate in connotation. "Religion" is one. For many, somehow, it has come to bring down the asbestos curtain. Luckily we can dodge that rough spot; our approach takes a different route. "Occultism" is another; but that need not alarm us, either. Occult merely means hidden—the thing beyond what we know. And that is itself the field of our projected exploration.

5

Corresponding roughly to these two aspects of psychics are two general classes of "schools." In one we find literally dozens of systems whose purpose is avowedly the development of "psychic powers." That means merely a degree of mechanical control over certain faculties latent in all of us, but as yet little understood. In these particular schools the "powers" are the main objective—communion with the dead, visions of the future, the obtaining of material benefits, and the like.

There also exist dozens of systems of a second type, some of them resembling superficially the first, but differing in one important respect: their stated aim is the development of the individual as a whole to the point where he can enter what amounts to another region of consciousness. It matters little what this region is called—the Universal, cosmic consciousness, Samadhi, God—or how it is approached. The objective is not various separate "powers" for their own sake, but a single state of mind.

Most of this latter group even go a step farther, and condemn all meddling with "psychics" as dangerous. In the not very distant past this attitude was probably justified. Today it is extreme. Certainly even the crudest psychic phenomena are, at the very least, legitimate materials for objective scientific study. In that case, of course, they should be allowed no more spiritual content than cosmic rays, or expanding nebulae, or the filterable viruses. The scientist's job is merely to establish their veridicity, to understand their nature, to construct an hypothesis of their action.

Toward this aspect of "psychics," it must be recognized, any other attitude is likely to be dangerous. It has often proved so. The dabbler gets results. Many of them are disconcerting. Many turn the seeker into by-paths apart from life, that lead into the queernesses of impractical, sometimes crazy, theories and cults. And even the best intentions in the world seem to be no safeguard. So true is this that, in merciful insulation, the average human is protected by an instinctive repulsion from the whole subject.

Nevertheless it is perfectly possible to start out comfortably and successfully with what are in reality "psychic" activities. This also has been proved. For some even, this may be the only effective method. And the fact remains, whatever route we elect for our approach to the high country, sooner or later we find ourselves utilizing some kind of "psychics." We come to an elevation where our ordinary workaday senses are not adequate. We have risen from the familiar solidities of the valley into a new kind of country. We are dealing with intangibles, and to deal with intangibles we are forced to work with psychic faculties. This is true in all cases. It is true even in the case of those philosophies and those individuals who are convinced that "psychics" are dangerous and deterrent and must be avoided. Their warnings are well-founded. But they are talking about something else. At the beginning they may avoid the direct approach through avowedly "psychic" methods; but as we gain altitude and approach the pass, the trails join.

In a previous volume—*The Betty Book*—I have told of Betty's first steps into this country beyond. In the following pages will appear some of her later explorations, together with my own first steps along the trail. So far we have been fortunate enough to avoid serious danger or distress. And on the journey we have come into possession of a compass—one which we feel can be trusted by others following this trail.

The basic difference between safety and danger, between anxiety and comfort, between surety and bewilderment is very simple. It is the aim. There are other factors along the way which we must anticipate and guard against, as will appear later. But we cannot do so unless, first of all, we know what we are after, and where we want to go. And we must refuse to be deflected. We must keep the aim single.

The primary nature of this aim, also, is very simple: we are headed for the high country of consciousness. If there are such things as "psychic powers," and if we early come into possession of them, it must be for use on our journey and for nothing else. If deliberately we undertake certain initial practices leading to any so-called "psychic state," it will be only as an aid to our greater intention, and for no other purpose, no matter how many other possible uses for them seem to offer themselves. As we penetrate the country beyond, many of these powers and conditions will come to us naturally and securely as a by-product of our progress. Others will as naturally fall into disuse, because they are crude and no longer necessary or effective. But meanwhile we must be vigilant neither to strain for their acquisition, nor to abuse the privilege of their possession. For it is when we make them ends in themselves, and collect or develop them for the sake of their power, that they become dangerous. They are staffs for our hands, not stunts for our gratification.

The same simple beginnings are common to either aim. The trail forks. There is a left- and a right-hand path. That the devices we use at the start may lead down the wrong trail as well as the right trail, is beside the point. So may any other device whatever, including the most direct form of communion possible to the mystic. We have our choice. And a good compass; which is our Aim.

*Now let us take up your attitude toward things you can't
understand. What is your first reaction? To make fun of
them. That is all right: nobody wants you not to have fun.
But it would be a better idea if you could make that your
second, or your third, or your fourth reaction, rather than
your first; provided that your first was that you want to
understand it. That would be a great help.*

*One more thing: Every day strengthen your desire for
understanding: every day make fertile your understanding
by moments of admitting eternal things to your consciousness.*

CHAPTER II

FAMILIAR GROUND

Young things are helpless. They must be fed, cared
for, protected until they mature through natural
growth. Then they must care for themselves. If not
permitted to do so, they deteriorate into fat parasitism.

In the animal world a compelling instinct thrusts the
fledgling from the nest as soon as it has grown its
feathers, severs the filial ties once the beast has learned
to use its teeth and claws. If occasionally, or with certain species, young and old stay together for a time, it is
not as a family, but rather as a co-operative unit in
which each, old and young, plays its equal and adult
part.

Man serves the same necessity. But in his case the instinct does not compel. He may inhibit it, or deny it. As
a parent he may cling to his child far beyond the time,
swayed sentimentally by misguided—and selfish—"affection," or more harshly by an egocentric demand of
filial obligation. Or it may be the child who lingers,
held by a wholly false sense of "duty." There is something to be said for him; but little for the youth who

9

lingers because he loves his safe comfort, or distrusts his ability to make his own way. There are plenty of them. They would not be permitted in the sure clean functioning of the animal world. The bird pushes the reluctant laggard over the edge of the nest.

It is a law, and a simple law: that of ripeness. When a seed—or an animal—or a man—is ripe, it must mature to its next phase. Or rot.

The impelling force behind that maturing is also simple. It is discontent. When the young thing has ripened, he becomes discontented, he wants to get out. Too often he is reproached as ungrateful, and is a grief to his parents who "have done everything for him." That is silly, for this is not discontent of captiousness, discontent against details. It is something more noble; rather a dissatisfaction with things as they are, with himself as he is. When we perceive clearly its significance, we turn the word inside out, and rename it ambition. Then it becomes admirable: but it is discontent just the same. And it can always be recognized because its state is of discomfort. Resentfully, always, we grope for comfort. We are yet to learn that comfort is not stable, but must be constantly recaptured.

As a race we follow that instinct fairly well. Whether we express it to ourselves or not, we do recognize that the fettered family is pathological. We approve the restlessness of ambitious youth. But curiously enough we fail to recognize exactly the same thing when it works on us in later years. When, at that time, the old formless unrest once again stirs our spirits—causelessly it may seem—we resent, or we endure. We have not learned this lesson of youth, which is that our discontents are among our most valuable gifts from life. They are not to be resented or endured. They are to be examined. And examination, if we are vitally intelligent, results in our doing something about it. Which, in

10

turn, means a new venturing. Curious that we can see this only in retrospect. Curious that we are able to smile so indulgently at the fevered blind rebellions of our adolescence, seeing them clearly for what they were, and yet fail to see that our present case is no different.

That was our emerging from our physical and mental adolescence. This can be our emerging from our spiritual adolescence. It can be a dangerous moment—or an inspiring one. It may close the door, or open it to a wide new land.

This happened to me a number of years ago. I could see no sense to it. My personal and material world should have been satisfactory. I was happily married; I had an interesting profession, in which I was successful; I was in excellent health, had independent means, congenial friends in all walks of life. Finally—most essential—I saw clearly plenty of work ahead and plenty of adventure opening up in certain projected excursions into a wilderness new to me. Certainly I had every ingredient for happiness. And I was happy, I told myself, entirely so! If, I asked myself, I were to be given a free hand to fashion a desirable life for myself, how could I improve on what I had? Nevertheless a faint uneasy restlessness—the restlessness that meets one on the far side of novelty—had begun to whisper in my ear. *Cui bono?* that miserable sneering question that awaits every one of us somewhere along the journey.

Fortunately for me, at this point I was led into a new venture. This experience I have tried to describe in another book *(The Betty Book)*, both as a factual story, and as an exposition of things learned through certain teachings. The latter seemed true and important to a few of us, and of general value. Nevertheless we wished to be pretty sure of that. We must try them out to see if

11

they would work. Pragmatism. As Dooley said: "Av it worruks, it's true." The only way to tell was to give them time to work. Therefore we delayed publication—for seventeen years.

Incidentally, I, personally, had to be driven to certain conclusions as to their origin. They purported to be given, through Betty, from outside Intelligences. We nicknamed them the Invisibles, largely because of their insistence on remaining anonymous.

For me that was rather a large order. Frankly I could not, for a long time, accept them for what they purported to be. But driven is the word: I was finally driven to it. It took a long time, and a gradual accumulation of small logicalities rather than large evidences—though these did not lack. Finally I could not reject them, simply because rejection at last became ridiculous. For each objection I had to adopt another explanation, and these perforce grew so numerous and so different that they in turn demanded a more inclusive explanation. And in the long run I found myself using such ingenious mental devices that they became more unbelievable than the thing itself. Just as I had my properly cautious skepticism all neatly arranged, along would come some other small fact that did not fit in anywhere. That too had to be explained, or the whole mess would fall down like a stack of matches. And to explain it altered the explanations of a lot of the others; and the new explanations had to be more and more ingenious or they would not fit, until it all got so complicated that anybody's most homespun reasoning would call it absurd. It was magnificent, but was it sense?

So, finally, that point was settled. I was willing to accept, as a fact, that we were receiving through Betty, from outside, and apparently discarnate, intelligences, a graded and progressing and logically acceptable instruction on how to get along in life.

Most of the ideas offered by these intelligences were foreign to my habit of thought. I will here epitomize from *The Betty Book* sufficient for the purpose of their basic concepts.

Filling all space, said they, is a great sea of undifferentiated force. We can call it life, or spirit, or the Universal—anything we please. But it is the thing by virtue of which all living things exist, through their ability to transmute this general force into something individual. In other words they—and we—are vital transformers. It follows that we are alive and developed in proportion to how much of this force we can accept, and how freely it flows through us. The better we do this the higher grade we occupy, and the more alive and contented and effective we become.

Ordinarily, said the Invisibles, this goes on unconsciously, and more or less inefficiently. We are self-contained. We are encrusted in a hard shell. A certain flow through us persists in spite of this. Otherwise we should not be alive at all. But too often it is the barest trickle: no more than sufficient to carry on painfully a slow progress and a torpid existence.

In the green stage of unripeness little can be done to alter these natural processes. But there comes a time, to everyone, when we can, if we will, take conscious and intelligent direction. Then these heretofore automatic processes will function not only better and more quickly, but less painfully. In *The Betty Book* I set down the philosophy and technique of how this can be done. It is unnecessary here to repeat more than basic principles. I will state them as briefly as possible.

One of these is that each of us occupies not only the physical body we see, but a second or spiritual body. This latter will continue to contain us after physical death. Though imperceptible to our ordinary senses, the spiritual body is no vague wraith of insubstantial shadow. It is perfectly real, made of definite substance, and will function in a world that corresponds to it. That world also is of definite substance. Indeed so far from the fuzzy or ghostlike is this world that, in one sense, its matter is even more substantial than that of the physical universe, for it interpenetrates—fills the interspaces—of the latter. In it the realities of consciousness will have more vivid scope than we know in our present phase. Through it the vital force of the universe acts more powerfully and directly than with us.

But—and here is the important point—that world is not separated from ours by a hard and fast iron wall of time. We can, in certain ways, begin to function in it now. Indeed at the time of ripeness that is what we must do if we are to continue efficient and developing. If we gain consciously and keep continuously our contact with it, our reservoirs will draw from unfailing abundance. The difference between that and our ordinary state would be the difference between power line and a storage battery.

In doing this our final aim is to develop a definite, close-knit core of self, in which we can have confidence as an indestructible unit. For only in this way can we be assured of a permanent nucleus of individuality which will hold securely together in the strain of life—and death.

Such are the barest of bare bones that upheld the body of the teachings we received. Their record now fills over two thousand pages. They cover a wide foreground of detail—as to how this force works in daily life; how consciously to seek it, and appropriate it, and apply it effectively. Incidental to the placing of that detail is an inclusive background of cosmology. The whole picture, background and foreground, is coherent; it is intellectually satisfying; it progresses both onward and upward until it escapes the grasp of our highest reaches of imagination. And it stands by itself, so that in the end it does not matter one bit when or from whom it came.

You've got to play with the idea before you can make it work, because you are not operating in your accustomed substance. You are employing a higher creative form which you don't know how to use, except unconsciously and relaxedly.

CHAPTER III

BORDER COUNTRY

Only a very dull man could receive such a body of such ideas without a wide shift in his point of view. Certainly I was not that dull. For one thing it gave me a rationale. It silenced my vague discontent. Here was a sufficing reason for being. I had a comfortable placement. That alone was worth while.

But it went further than that. I began to see things whole, to discern—not too clearly at first—a general scheme. Things fitted together. Certain of them lost importance; such as death, hatreds, irritations, conflicts, antagonisms, to mention a few at random. Certain others gained importance—the small acts, efforts, and decisions of the minutes and hours of every day. How should they not, if one is *shown* that the causes and effects of life are not isolated, but smoothly continuous? That they come to no dead ends, that there are no dead ends, not even death itself?

That was all to the good. It sorted me out mentally. One goes ahead more confidently if he does not have to go it blind. Indeed so heartening is this one little item of intellectual understanding that for some time I was quite content. This much demonstrated, in my own case, that the thing did work, and that because of it I was getting along in life with greater satisfaction.

But shortly it was borne in on me that the mental was

16

only a part. Betty, and a few others, were getting something else out of it. They had the same mental understanding as I, but also something more, a relationship of some kind that so far I had missed.

I had insight enough to recognize in this a tie-in with all the other "systems" of illumination and advancement into which human instinct has groped. There have been many. Sometimes they have been dignified into religions. Sometimes they have been limited down into philosophies, or merely into cults. But whatever they were, their adherents fall invariably into two classes: those who gave mental assent and who, in return gained a certain—often valuable—understanding; and those who came into some closer relationship that brought them the something more. And no matter what the "system" was, it worked, and endured, if that relationship was established. It remained merely an interesting philosophy if that relationship was missed.

My insight penetrated just this far, and no deeper. What was this peculiar relationship, and how did one enter into it? That was what I must try to find out.

My whole training was against me. I was, as yet, interested only in definite, clear-cut ideas. All my experience, up to now, seemed to have proved them the most reliable guides. At any rate they were least likely to conduct one into dangerous fogs. I rather prided myself on being practical and hardheaded and "intellectual." What I wanted was direct statements, ideas, scientific facts. And I demanded them. I set out to pin down these supposed Invisibles.

Well, I got definite statements at times, especially in the beginning. But somehow I felt discontented, though I could not quite place my finger on the why. It was as though these people had some idea or purpose

17

that they kept withholding, something below the obvious plain surface of what they said. I sensed it constantly, as one senses the hum behind a long-distance conversation. It was subtle, and baffling, and finally it got on my nerves. I demanded a showdown. Why don't you *say*, in so many words, what you mean? said I. I'm an intelligent human being; I can understand plain speech. Here, from the record, is the verbatim discussion:*

Invisible: Please note: you will not get scientific explanation such as you expect. You will get the *reality* as we can manage to give it, which you can deduce as theory later. We cannot tell you in words which would convey anything to you, what we must accomplish by molding you to the thing itself. It becomes increasingly difficult to put things so as to be easily acceptable to your intellect. Understanding can be acquired only by actual participation in the reality. At present there is no reaction of experience to words representing that reality.

Stewart: Nevertheless words will be necessary to explain to others who have not experienced the reality.

Invisible: That will be your part after the perception is yours—after you are capable of entering it in reality. Only through your capacity of understanding can truth be produced in written symbol. It is impossible for us alone. From the beginning that has been difficult for you to realize. Reckon on statements as near as we are capable of making them; but only as an accompani-

---

* For the benefit of those who have not read *The Betty Book*, it should be explained that these records were dictated to me by Betty while in a kind of disassociated state—not, however, amounting to unconsciousness. Sometimes she spoke in her own person; sometimes one of the Invisibles spoke through her, the shift being marked by a change in voice, diction and style.

ment to the acquisition of the thing itself. Without the latter, explanations would be sterile.

Stewart: As I understand it, then, it is impossible for you to express major truths in words; but after you lead us into the reality, it is within our power to find the words that will express and prove it.

Invisible: That's better; that's much better. You kind of broke through then. That cleared up things considerably.

Stewart: I don't see why you did not say that before.

Invisible: You acquired it—produced it yourself.

Stewart: But it seems a simple enough intellectual idea....

Invisible: No, not an intellectual idea. It is a growth in yourself. It would have remained a sterile intellectual idea, as you call it, unless we had forced you to produce it yourself.

Stewart: But it could have been stated....

Invisible: Why will you have only one dimension! But have patience with our methods. They are more far-seeing in results than you imagine. For the present don't try to acquire too definite a formula in your medium, but work for comprehension of the thing in ours. The difference is between the taking of detached, intellectual, occasionally contemplated concepts, and having them a constant, integral part of your consciousness. This difference is the most difficult to present simply to the educated. Minds which are firmly established in their own sphere of action will not even pause to contemplate another. It is the keystone of the whole benefit to be derived from any of these teachings, and is always impatiently acknowledged and instantly rejected because it dethrones the sovereignty of the lesser instrument receiving the message.

Betty: How stiff words are! They've only got one plane—like paper dolls instead of people. Takes so

19

many of them. Leave it: it's getting all daubed up with words. So we'll leave that.

This did jar me ahead a little. At least I had a new intellectual conception. I had a new sequence, a new pattern: that while pure reason has its function in this kind of exploration, it is not an *originating* function. It acts *after* the fact, rather than before. It does not itself find anything; it thinks about things after they are found. Then it can appraise, accept or reject, utilize, apply—but only what is brought to it by other, and perhaps higher, aspects of mind.

That was an advance. But I must have been, I can see now, an exasperating sort of pupil. I had not yet decided just how literally Betty's experiences should be taken. *Somebody* had to keep his feet solidly on the ground! And I had to be the one. Therefore, as I saw it, I could not lay aside my tried and tested reasoning powers in favor of something that looked to me pretty vague and nebulous. And I said so.

"Do not," advised the Invisibles, "be abashed by your ponderable mind, any more than you are abashed by ponderable people. There is, you know, a certain type of over-sane, over-cautious people who have never sensed intangible verities; who prefer to occupy themselves exclusively with the more limited ponderables; just as there are the unfortunates who have never sensed the rapture of a perfume or the ecstasy of a color harmony. Escape frequently from the limitations of your ponderable mind, and capture a small boy's enjoyment in constructing yourself a tree house, high above your ordinary workaday dwelling place."

"Your advice appeals to me," I agreed, "but it reminds me a little of the Book of Etiquette: 'When meeting new people always assume an easy uncon-

20

scious demeanor.' Suppose you have an idea in the back of your mind that perhaps you are only going to make a chump of yourself. Just how do you recommend getting round that?"

"You can," they replied quaintly, "begin to gain this reality without believing in it at all! All we ask of anybody at first is an attitude of receptivity. The intellectual attitude doesn't matter, not in the least. Consider a flower in need of sunlight—a flower possessed of thinking intelligence. Can't get sunlight in its heart unless it opens its petals. If it opens its petals, it gets sunlight, and the sunlight has its effect. Now why should a gardener, interested principally in the growth of flowers, care a hang whether that flower's theory of why it opened is that it possesses a subconscious and illusory sun, or not? Whether it imagines that a gardener exists or not, provided it opens its petals?

"Now we do not care whether we are labelled Subconscious Secundus or Subconscious Tertius; or whether anybody thinks some portion of his personality evokes these experiences, or that they are an independent reality. If you entertain in an attitude of receptivity what comes to you, you are receiving the sunlight, and that must have its effect in development. What dust and chaff comes to you at the same time will be disposed of and pass away. By maintaining the willingness to receive—not to criticize at first—that which is intrinsically true will insensibly become part of you, and you will ultimately and most unexpectedly find yourself possessed of a belief that will be a certainty.

"This does not mean that one should try to accept unquestioningly, nor that he should inanely refuse intellectual examination. It merely means the aforementioned willingness to receive and place on file for future reference, so to speak, what cannot immediately be accepted. It implies a willingness to leave the question

21

open; neither to seek for far-fetched explanation nor to attempt an unripe credence.

"If quite honestly one can do this—with entire self-honesty—the event can safely be left to—I was going to say 'us,' but I will say time. You see 'us' *may* be Sub-conscious Sub-one or Sub-two."

I have a great plea to make. I want you to come with me, all of you who are ready. I want you to lay aside all effort at understanding and interpretation, and come out into the great outside. There is only one way to do it. Just say to yourselves: I will lay aside the symbols for the reality. I will be like a mere plant, responsive to unwordable influences. My busy, near-sighted little self must be quieted, set aside for the purpose of expanding a great and dormant faculty within me. This faculty is weak; it barely records impressions yet; but through it surges all that is enduring.

CHAPTER IV

PIONEER METHODS

Curious how we acquire wisdom! Over and over again the same truth is thrust under our very noses. We encounter it in action; we are admonished of it; we read it in the written word. We suffer the experience; we graciously assent to the advice; we approve, intellectually, the written word. But nothing happens inside us.

Then one day some trivial experience or word or encounter stops us short. A gleam of illumination penetrates the depth of our consciousness. We see! Usually it is but a glimpse; but on rare occasion a brilliant flash reveals truth fully formed. And we marvel that this understanding has escaped us so long.

For months, literally, the Invisibles hammered away at my dullness. Not that I occupied the whole stage of their attention! They had Betty's education to attend to; and there was also the structure of the teachings to be defined. But I was part of the job; and they kept at me. And always the same line of attack.

"Make the leap," they urged. "Dare to do it. Take a chance on our being right. You cannot connect up in an unbroken series of steps with what you know. This reality is not on the outskirts; a gap must be bridged. Lay aside at intervals the measuring stick of your mind. It is very necessary to employ the measuring stick ordinarily; but lay it aside intermittently. Hurl yourself into space, as it were. It will not hurt you to go bravely out to pick up a clue or two. You've been trying to creep up on things on the scientific side, but they've got to be boldly taken, artistically, in the present case. Conservatism travels so slowly. Radicalism suffers for its blunders, but arrives with force.''

Here Betty took up the discourse: ''Anything gorgeous and wonderful could happen to you if only you'd have the courage to ignore and outdistance your ordinary restricted self. Everybody who has pioneered has thrown aside the customary routine and hurled himself at one inspired ideal.

''The way I want to go about it seems so opposed to that scientific slow-freight kind of feeling. I don't suppose you could make the world credit anybody who went around leaping toward things; but the leap is an ingredient, and you can't go ahead without making it. When you leave out the leap you are not working in the nature of the substance. You are trying to work in the new substance with the nature of the old. You can't do it, except slowly and painfully.

''That's the new big conception we've got to grow around—this idea of working in the nature of the substance. They are trying to percolate this to us. It's the next phase of our work. We've gone as far as we can without acquiring it.

''I suppose there's a striking and sensible way to say it, because I can *feel* the mechanical explanation of it. There's undoubtedly a mechanical explanation that fits it. I don't know mechanics.''

She paused a moment, then chuckled. ''So childish!

24

They put legs on a flying machine and make it walk around!''

"We are trying," continued the Invisible, "to drag you out of your restricted element, to show you the taking off process: how to zoom. You can't conquer the air by working the levers on the ground. It is only by utilizing the attributes of the new substance that you can succeed. This next big conception of how to function spiritually is only to be accomplished by taking seriously this leaping process."

This was the time I woke up. That phrase "working in the nature of the substance" rang a bell somewhere in the back of my mind.

It happened that at just that time I was taking my first steps in learning the great game of golf. I early found there are plenty of good books on how to play it. And that each month a number of magazines tell it all over again. Nothing has been more carefully dissected and described than the mechanics of the golf swing. And there can be no doubt that all this careful analysis is a great help. A man at least knows what he is to go after, and that is a lot better than just going it blind. But nobody ever learned to play golf in his armchair. We've got to go and do it.

Simple and obvious! But it was my own private illumination in this matter. Reading about golf gets the thing only in the mind. But when I got out on the practice tee and swung a club, I was translating this idea into actual objective material—I was bringing it into being in the physical substance of my body. In the one case I had only an idea, in the other I had an actual *sensation:* a subjective *feeling:* inside myself. It was something like the difference between the blueprint of a house and the house itself.

Go out and do it: that was the answer. Not think about it; but do it and get the feel of it—whatever this reality was that the Invisibles kept talking about. And suddenly it occurred to me that it is certainly more fun to get out and play golf than to sit at home and read about it.

Agreed. But how to make a start? One has to have implements, tools, some sort of instructions to go with them. The Invisibles obliged; but by no means with a full set. They never do. But they did give me a handhold.

"You must gain it in imagination first," said they, "and then work back through slow steps to connect it with observed facts. Analyze the process of education through mentality, the gradual progressive formation within the minds of children of the accumulated knowledge of the race. Take, for example, the grasping of the idea of evolution, or what is known as the solar system. Such things can be successfully presented only through the imagination—the only function that reaches into the realms that are intangible, but nevertheless facts of civilization. Having analyzed this process, apply it to the spiritual education. Reach the imagination into the reality we present. It can only be made tangible, established within you, by this type of personal experiment."

"I don't think," Betty interjected, "that's a very good word—imagination. It's too cobwebby with unrealities."

"Imagination?" they cried, astonished. "Why, that is the very *gateway* to reality! Imagination is the Power of Transportation—that overrides space and time! Imagination enables you to put yourself *anywhere*. It's the power of juxtaposition, that puts together things

26

that were never put together before, at points of contact that nobody else ever thought of. It's the power to see the Pattern.

"You call it a plaything. You've always called it a plaything. But actually it's the one thing you possess that connects you with the next substance. It's a transmuting chemical. We will hunt for a word that will be more solidly respectable than imagination. Call it speculative philosophy, if you prefer. Give it any vestment of dignity, but utilize it to connect with what is beyond your experience, beyond the limits of your present conceptions."

"It seems to me," I objected, "that imagining things has got a lot of people into trouble."

"Failures do not affect the law," they pointed out. "Do not fear the strength of the gift because it has been misused. In looking at failures, take them as valuable warnings; but negatives, not positives."

There was a pause, and then Betty said, "Well, while I'm laid aside, what else? I have an unhooked feeling this way."

She was silent a moment as though awaiting orders. Then in a puzzled tone: "Such a bulk of unrecognized law!"

For several minutes she seemed to study this. Finally: "I can't go into that bulk: I can apparently feel quite comfortable near it and around it, but there is no comprehension in my mind of it, except bit by bit. I know lots of things, but I can't teach myself them. I want to go now with myself that knows things. It's nice not to try to understand—just to know."

I am heir of eternal expansion and clothed in my right to partake of it. Oh, do not ever again let me be poor-spirited or faded or gnarled in form! I want the richly patterned life. I want to be gorgeously spirited, I want the ceremonial beauty and fragrance of the spirit. I want the freedom of its force. I want the quiet whispering of its wisdom. I want the simplicity of its love. Oh help me to the fullness of life! I pray for the fullness of life with an undivided heart, so that I may rest absorbing strength, not emptying myself of life!

CHAPTER V

THE JUMPING-OFF PLACE

We occupy habitually but a limited portion of the consciousness we already possess. Not so long ago we were unwilling to admit that such uninhabited areas existed at all. Most of us just occupied the ordinary territories of our thoughts and emotions and sensations, and were satisfied to let it go at that. But latterly even the cautious scientists have come to recognize and study the subconscious, the superconscious, intuition, inspiration, hypnotism—a lot of things outside the snug stockade of our comfortable habit. To be sure, most of these outlying areas, and the dwellers therein, still have somewhat of a bad name. And possibly a few of them deserve it. Nevertheless they are being increasingly acknowledged as a wide borderland country, already within our reach, extending into the unknown far beyond the mark set by our accustomed "limitations."

"The great value of an interest in these things," said the Invisibles, "of at least admitting their *possibility*, is that it affords an extendible frontier. The inspiration to explore and acquire and administer new territories of life is always ahead as a lure.

"Youth lives entirely on this frontier, though more on its physical counterpart, exploring the sensuous possibilities. That is one of the secrets of its enthusiasm and rapid development. Undamaged by misuse, this faculty should persist, arriving at maturity with a healthy appetite for the next stage—spiritual development. Hard and fast boundaries, such as those set by the phase through which popular scientific interpretation is passing—your true scientist is not that way—are very restricting and disheartening. As a result, you make no effort toward liberation into the higher sensations which lead toward ultimate reality. You are left flattened on top, confined by the mechanics of your minds."

After all we ourselves set those boundary markers, arbitrarily. We put them at the limits of visibility, as far as we could see from our present stockade of accustomed life. And abandoned them, taking for granted that they are accurately placed.

That is peculiar, seeing that mere curiosity takes us over most sky-lines. But for some reason this looks dubious to us. We can look back and see clearly our path of evolution, like a broad highway behind us. But mists roll across the future, and its forms are half-glimpsed. Perhaps we are a little feared of the venturing.

Nevertheless it is in that direction we must travel. These present comfortable headquarters are not permanent. Ultimately they must be out there somewhere, in the dimness. It would seem only common sense, then, to scout out the new site. Perhaps we may like it. Perhaps we may even want to go up and occupy. We can always back-track.

These ideas came to me gradually, a few at a time. It was their realization that finally persuaded me to explore this frontier country myself, in person. Only in

29

that way, I decided, could I satisfy myself as to what it was all about. Then I would be in a position to form my own opinion, instead of depending on hearsay and guesswork.

But the actual setting out, when at last I faced it seriously, presented a number of unexpected problems. The trouble was not in getting advice—I found plenty of guidebooks filled with that—but to figure out what not to take. Spiritual development, I had come to realize, is individual. No two men are alike, from thumb print to immortal soul. There are no shotgun prescriptions, whether of cult, philosophy or religion. We cannot be helped by rigid regimes. We must have direction, not directions. What is desirable? Which way points our compass? What, in clearer definition, are we after? That is about all we can be told. Recognizable signposts can be planted for us toward the high country, but we alone must find our own paths. And if we expect more detailed guidance, we plan for confusion.

My own landmarks were revealed to me by Betty's reports of her explorations. Just at first, I admit, some of these were a cropful. Great sweeps of gorgeousness were never my line. I like things tacked down to something solid—by at least one corner. But I hung on hopefully, and after a while things began to make sense. In the meantime my feeling for mystery and adventure were vastly stimulated.

In the next chapter I shall quote some of these reports. Taken as a whole, I believe, they combine to place the main features of the most accessible territory in this new country. This does not mean that they are the only features; or even that they are the ones we shall first discern. They give a hint of what, sooner or later, we may all look forward to there—but not necessarily a promise.

"There is no use," warned the Invisibles, "in previsioning or predicting what this higher consciousness will accomplish or perceive. That is entirely individual and temperamental. An indication of the things which one may acquire is all that can be given from one to another."

What degrees of "reality," as we use the word, Betty's reported experiences represented, it is difficult to say. Sometimes they seem to have been actual excursions into another condition of life. Sometimes they were obviously symbolic, weaving a gorgeous and sustaining richness, like a colorful orchestration, beneath the simple pure theme of reality. But whether "real" or not, these experiences all combined to lead surely and definitely into reality. And for twenty years that reality has withstood the test of daily living.

My directions, up to this time, really boiled down to one thing: in order to approach Betty's new "substance" or region of consciousness or whatever it was, I was to use my imagination as a kind of magic carpet. By wholeheartedly picturing to myself the general conditions described by Betty, I was to draw nearer to the thing itself—prepare myself, so to speak, for eventual participation. Also, as a kind of corollary, I must take a recess from the intellect and its criticisms. A recess, not a divorce. For the time being I was to be wholly irresponsible of what the intellect might have to say about the matter; to be—for the time being—wholly wild and extravagant; willing to accept things I did not know about as though they were really so.

"It is curious how you have to take the things they give," said Betty. "I hold an idea rather loosely when I get it. I take it as I would take the beauty of the rainbow. I know I cannot hold it or reach it or even look at it closely. I know I can't, and so I don't try. That is the way I take these big ideas in the beginning—somewhat like the rainbow. I remember them wholly; but they are out of my reach in the analysis, the pulling of them to pieces to explain them.

"You know, a child's first impulse, when you give it a beautiful flower, is to pull it to pieces. That is natural enough, but a flower is not to be handled that way. It is to be enjoyed whole, as an inspirational thing. These foreshadowed ideas also are delicate things, blossoming things. They must have more effect on the inspirational side, and less in concentration on pulling them to pieces to understand. The dissecting of them is only allowable after the flower influence, or the rainbow influence, has entered into you.

"So many beautiful things are put into the world solely to help you make the jump-off. I took the rainbow because it seems so obviously inaccessible that no one could dream of spoiling it by grasping and analyzing it. You must not starve that rainbow side. It is more practical than you think. It is the mechanism of liberation."

How do I function in the universal strength? How does a bird hold itself up in the air, resting its wings confidently on the air currents. How do you hold yourself up in the water, abandoning yourself to its support. How do I hold myself here? By amalgamation of my heart's desire with the strength that is myself and not myself. I lie individually quiescent in it, as one floats contentedly in the great ocean.

CHAPTER VI

LANDMARKS

In a new country a man must find his own way. The landmarks planted by his predecessors he must discover for himself. When he overtakes them, he is heartened by their evidence that others have passed this way and found the way reliable. That is the principal reason for placing landmarks, against the time when someone shall need them.

But also there is a value in travelers' tales. They excite interest. They breathe the atmosphere of adventure in strange lands. They awaken the romance of the unexplored and the unknown, arousing us to venture.

Before commencing the records of Betty's explorations I must emphasize one thing that every writer knows. No account does more than insignificant credit to the original. And this seems to be particularly true when we deal with the far reaches of the mind. A kind of penumbra of illumination accompanies the thing itself, which is lacking to the record of cold type. I suppose this is inevitable when we concern ourselves with a reality whose greater part is intangible, beyond the measuring ability of the brain. I cannot sufficiently stress this apparently obvious statement. Only personal experience can realize its import.

33

This penumbra, then, must be left to the reader's imagination, together with the actual physical setting: Betty lies blindfolded on the couch; I sit at my table, pencil in hand, taking down her words.

Betty: I am in a garden with a clipped hedge around it, and an arched gateway. I don't know why I am here....

Now I'm passing through the gate, leaving behind the green and blooming garden. Before me is a desert country, but the soil is rich and unfed-upon. It just needs a gardener, that's all, to extend the cultivated territory, making it beautiful and appreciated and desired by man....

We are going to bring this new region to life, so that it can be occupied and extended by others. It won't have any hedge at the end of it. It's going to run out into the pauseful shadows of ruminating trees, which will be the boundaries of contemplation around our garden. People will come into it in contemplation for entering and mastering the wilderness beyond. It will be a beautiful inspirational place; not like a clipped hedge on the boundaries of thought....

That's rather a pity, I think, for I've always liked clipped hedges, and the feeling of living behind them, sheltered and contented. But never mind: it's just a shred of regret for something comfortable and accustomed....

It's all gone now.

(Pause.)

Invisible: Supposing that all your conscious life you had been imprisoned in a box, and all you knew was the interior of that box; and suddenly you were released and found you could mingle with the world surrounding it. How would you explain it to the occupants of the interior? Wouldn't you try to make them expand in imagination, surround in comprehension their present limitations in preparation for release? (Pause.)

Betty: Now I seem to contain my former self as something I've swallowed....I'm completely outside the box ....I've got to give way to this feeling, and it will explain itself in time.

Invisible: It's quite simple. It's like being hatched. (Pause.)

Betty: I'm struggling with comprehension.

Invisible: The vortex of relaxation is simply breaking your shell and releasing you into the surrounding life. Don't you see the difference of conditions? How obviously the greater powers of the surrounding life are to yours as the world is to the interior of an egg? It is hopeless to compress and reduce it for you. We must release you into it so it can explain itself.

Betty: I am not free to function in it. I can only sense it; trying to struggle to consciousness in the new element.

Invisible: Recollect that this is hard pioneer work, bit by bit, a struggle to conquer the wilderness of lack of comprehension. Even if it seems fantastic to you, or obvious, or unproductive, live with this idea of surrounding yourself. Store it away to ripen. It will shake down into place.

(Pause.)

Betty: Rebirths are going on all about us, and we pay no attention. They are such commonplaces. Mosquitoes from wrigglers, that get their wings atop the water—all kinds of metamorphoses. I don't know why it should surprise me so to stick my head up into a new world, and realize that I can gradually draw myself up until I get entirely into it. It is quite natural.

Betty: I just work hard, and then I find I am raised up somehow to a superstate, and am in touch with something I did not have before; and I see it vaguely and look back and tell you about it. But I *do* it, whatever I'm at. That's why I work so hard and keep quiet so long. I'm gaining a sense of reality, experiencing, doing; instead of just reflecting. That means I've got actually to work in this living beyondness and absorb into the unconscious, as you call it, until I have something to produce in the conscious....

Now I'm here; and the other is vague and unsubstantial....I am functioning as a half-conscious newborn thing, but in a world real enough to stamp on, to expand into definitely with the strange new powers that are urging within me. In the quiet, dimly perceived as yet, my extended self senses great desires. Beauty's new functions and satisfactions are surrounding me. I am too weak to grasp them. I can't even tell you about what I do grasp: it's too delicate for formulation....

You know what the extent and possibilities are of the intellectual life. Its vast joys and discoveries are the dry bones of this other region of life. This is the vibrant embodiment of what the intellectual imagination dimly shadows. It would inspire the respect of any angle of learning: the scholar, the intellectualist, the psychologist, the observers and searchers in any quarter. The bigness of its possibilities are untranslatable. It is as impossible to put them into words as it is to put the ocean in a bucket. Nevertheless I must bring back some of it in some fashion. If I went on a visit and had a great experience, I'd try to tell you about it....

Now I want to enjoy the continuous rhythm of it a little while. It is so beautiful: it's all like music....

I said music, didn't I? But I'm not sure what it is that enters me and rearranges my particles and transmutes and strengthens and makes me so happy. It has such a rearranging and ordering of you....

It would sound silly if I said anything it was like: It is

36

so tremendous. I should say it was the perfect ordering of all elements, an exquisite joy of participating in harmony. My own little joy of life is welded to that of every other harmonized being. I've forgotten my individual part: I'm in a great chorus. I should think you would feel the swell of it....

(Chuckled.)

I feel like a tramp stealing a ride under a car and suddenly asked into a Pullman....Wonderful, to be a part, even a little part of anything that moves on with such majesty and beauty and power....

But I've got to say good-bye....I've enjoyed myself *so* much. It's been more like being honored than instructed today. I should like to be more susceptible to that ordering rhythm I called music. There are so many things in this consciousness that are beautiful—so many things I participate in without understanding. Something like being a dog: his associations with higher beings are very satisfactory and intensely desirable, but he doesn't altogether comprehend them. He just enjoys them.

Betty: I'll keep still and make this out now....Putting me to sleep....I'm traveling....There are people around me....

I've discovered something...a method of travel; I've stumbled on it....I've been in this room before; kitchen and dining room....Now I'm going away....I'm on a balcony...I'm with M....

Ugh! That looks so uncomfortable, like a fungus growth. It is a horrid-looking thing. She has fed it for so long; now it eats her....

That's curious; that's the thing that accompanies everybody. Supposing everything you'd done or thought, the *tendency* of your life, had a shape; as if your days were bricks and you had built something. And suppose your eyes were adjusted so that you could see what everybody had built. That is vaguely what I mean when I say people are walking around with a thing that accompanies them: that is the way I see people here. It is a pleasure to see them when they have a balanced growth straight ahead, instead of one of those fungus growths.

Stewart: What was that dining room and kitchen and balcony stuff?

Betty: That's where I traveled. In stretching my spiritual body I stumbled on an outlet.

Stewart: Why travel there?

Betty: That just happened. It sounds crazy to see people that way; and to travel around to see them but that's what I did.

It makes the world seem so small when you reach out for people, and the space between somehow shuts up like a telescope. I don't understand that. Got to do some experimenting around. I don't see how you can pull out and push in space like that....

Why, how astonishingly near that brings things! Isn't that astonishing! Why, *isn't* that astonishing! Even the distance to the other consciousness is not distance of space; it's a slowness or torpidity in penetrating. It's just lack of the right combination that makes it seem distant. It is so *near* when you clear that intervening denseness which is not space....

How can I tell this? Supposing I was in a dark room, and then a bright light was turned on. The darkness and the light occupy the same area, don't they? One overcomes the other and reveals what the other did not. Well, instead of being in the dark substance of consciousness, I'm in the brighter revealing one. Density is gone. I'm in the same place I was, but with greater vision.

It is all One; Here; Now—all the heavens and hells and universes superimposed. Why, that is perfectly tremendous! It gets nearer and nearer until it all seems right on top of me! More and more revealing light!...

I can't pierce it further. I'm not big enough: it would overwhelm me and burst me. I can't do it....

I'm a little tired and shaken with that big effort. It was as though I became merely a container for something that entered. It was a curiously powerful sensation, but I didn't quite grasp it....

I'm coming back now....I feel the way an electric light bulb does when it is turned off: all empty and dark!

Betty: I don't believe it will be possible to tell you yet of the dimension I am in: I understand so little....

Supposing, to start with, I presage it to you as an entirely new atmosphere. In it I am perfectly vigorous and strong and conscious, but I am all sympathetic. That is, I have a universal sense, not only of myself alone, but as if all the others were part of the atmosphere. Our usual atmosphere is a lot of little separate cells—Tom's, Dick's and Harry's—all more or less attracting or repelling or self-seeking. This new atmosphere contains them all dissolved, as it were, into one fluid substance. It's like possessing a bigger body, instead of being a separate atom of a body. I can see how you contract your vision in proportion as you become a little Tom-Dick-or-Harry cell; or how you expand it in proportion as you live in the atmosphere that contains them all as part of a great universal life.

I've made an awful mess trying to tell you. I've said it badly because I gave the impression of a merging of individualities. It is not that. They are distinct; but it's the merging of the substance possessed by all of them that produces the magic....

It is drifting away from me now. I am slipping back into the restricted little egotistical consciousness, the atmosphere of diminished vision. Little by little I slide right on down, seeing smaller and smaller aspects, watching each person's blindness and disease and low-grade effort magnify itself to the proportions of a walled world of its own.

What a stupid thing!

Betty: I'm having a delightful and mysterious time enjoying new sensations. Somebody's making me do things; things that are a great elation. Pretty soon I'll understand them and tell you. But I can't tell you in *petit-point* language; I can just work in big influence—the way clouds travel....

All the destiny and isolation of ordinary life is dispersed. I am stripped of something that sets apart from participation in all-surrounding life; and, fantastic as it may sound, I am so susceptible, capable of interchange, that it is as if I were made of blotting paper, only with a power of rejection if I choose. It is very real, and very pleasant to be so out in the cosmos. It is only little mean mundane fear that would make me worry about individuality. I don't worry. There's just a shred of an idea that individuality ought to be tended to....

Why! That's a new idea! Only I can't explain it. The word "love" doesn't suit my needs; I'll pass it by. I must gather something expressing more vigorous action, less fuzzed up with individuality....

I'm doing something quite astonishing. There are influences around me radiating the warmth of human affection, only with so much greater power. I dissolve to their love; I surround them as they surround me, steeping in each other's heart-expansion. It's so transforming, breath-taking, and I can't tell you in words.

Now, the strange thing is, I reach out and spread around each one I care for, this atmosphere. And as more and more people are brought in and each adds his contribution to the atmosphere, it enlarges and grows stronger and becomes firm, like a continent in a surrounding ocean.

I don't understand the rest very well. I seem actually to *be* that firm body—I feel it in all its parts—and yet it is composed of many people. How can that be?

Invisible: It is not easy to sit down to a comprehension of universality. Only dimly can you sense it as the great ocean connecting all the islands and continents. This element of the interstices we will name universal in an effort to set it down simply. All the parceled-off objective things, of however great magnitude, are but the islands and continents among and around which flows the great common carrier of universal spirit.

Betty: I must start over in different words. Wait a minute. I'll start on the other side: I'll be the ocean....

Now I am. I am the ocean, the ether, the all-surrounding substance in which individuals are suspended. It's like a universal contribution from all hearts. It's not that I, mightier, surround the various personalities floating in the great ocean, but that each meets me there. Each, through the functions of his being, sends out a quality capable, worthy of entering this substance, this universal ocean. He can withdraw it; he still is an individual. But when he sends it forth, it is his highest potentiality. All consciousness is open to him. He passes into what we can only call godship. Only by collecting a group of your dearest, going forth with your heart among them, cementing, as it were, a collective entity, and continually enlarging it, putting forth the substance among you, can you start toward comprehension of the Universal Consciousness.

Invisible: How can we make you desire, be eager for

41

the delights of this connective consciousness? It is as hopeless as trying to tell a little child in its sand box how much fun it is to be grown-up and married. And yet there is no other acquisition of life in the way of grown-upness that compares with this faculty.

Betty: (After a pause.) I am trying to get it into a mechanism which will stabilize it as a reality to you: a definite acquirable process, not a mere imagery....

Each time I unite myself with someone or something in eagerness of admiration and affection—by that process I have merged momentarily with the Universal. That is clear. But also there seem to be definite steps reaching to the conscious use of this universal process: response, admiration, adoration, to unity. This gradual lessening of separateness from the thing admired eventually makes it possible to draw from it its spiritual essence, feeding upon it as it were. Then you can produce your own interpretation, your own embodiment of this essence....

Anyway I know now what that phrase means: God is love. It always sounded so strained and affected to me. I don't like it yet; but that is my stupidity. At least I know what it means. There are so many word seeds we don't know how to plant and make grow into life-giving things!

Betty: (After a long interval.) I am trying to grow into the size of this place I've come to....

When you are very cold and enter a warm room, you say to yourself that you are in a different atmosphere, and expand to it. That is the difference between ordinary life and the element I'm in.

Invisible: Supposing you had always been of the general buoyancy of a flatiron, and then suddenly someone showed you how, by continuously opening yourself up, you could become more like a balloon. Very little difference, you see, between you and the air. You became simply an envelope for it, taking the certain amount of it which differentiates you.

Now substitute for that substance contained inside the balloon—which also supports it outside—the universal quality of life. You feel it everywhere, in the woods and the waters, the endless manifestations of vitality, pulsing and vibrating in contrast to the inanimate things you handle so constantly. Try to see what this life actually is like in essence, and not in its varied forms. Then realize this: when you can associate yourself enough with this quality consciously to rest in it, depend upon it, like the balloon—then the great secret of these teachings is yours.

The widest happiness and greatest vigor is to be obtained in acquiring this faith in the life-substance. It gives you a simple concept of support and endowment.

(Pause.)

Betty: How delightful this upholding life-substance is! It is so marvelously happy and natural. I think it is mostly the freedom of it that impresses me. It extends in every direction there is—and there seem to be some new directions. There is no strain or sanctimonious struggle for unified feeling: it is just magnitude and simplicity. I can't get out of it; I can't get around it: I can't fall off; I can't stand on it. It is a supporting universal thing beyond our conception....

I suppose for a moment I am being held in a perfect balance of some kind; unattainable ordinarily, but permitted as an ideal....

The minute I stop, the thing that impresses me is the tingling vitality of it. There is nothing passive about it; you couldn't hang back in it. You might be in perfect repose, but you couldn't be dead in it....

I keep quiet, and I breathe away the barriers between

the two consciousnesses, and I think that I hold the actual golden essence of this vitality with which we buy our happiness; but I can't bring it back. It slips through my fingers. I am not built so I can hold it. It is like gasoline going through a chamois skin.

Betty: I'm back again where I was the other day, only I'm seeing it a little more clearly.

(Long pause.)

I never knew such repose and power and self-produced rapture existed, such freedom, such immensity of happiness. I say 'self-produced' because it need not be blindly, spasmodically found in a fleeting condition. Its laws can be understood, making it possible to continue to live in it. My own understanding of those laws started long ago with the physical relaxation. That was the first step. That released the tension and allowed my higher powers to grow and expand and acquire knowledge of themselves. And now I hesitate to use the word relaxation any longer in connection with this great life-consciousness and energy....

I am like a powerful machine in perfect running order, but what the mechanics call "idling." What I am trying to get at is the idea of the condition I'm experiencing. Loafing isn't it; it has too perfect preparedness and readiness. Yet it is not keyed up, either, but in equilibrium. I am so conscious of repose and receptivity, but the effect is entirely different, in its feeling of strength, from all the words I know, such as relaxation, rest, vacation....

While I'm vibrating with this power, nothing of a damaging nature can affect me. I can handle it uncontaminated or unpermeated by it. What would be grave disturbances to me in lower levels, now seem merely opportunities for a selection of life. I can't actually discard the disturbances, but I surround them with a wholesomeness that makes them innocuous.

Invisible: This control, this acquisition of raised vibrations—whatever you choose to call it—is absolutely within the desire of the individual. If you really want it, nothing from the outside can more than momentarily distract. It is a thing that one builds or does not build, according to his caliber.

(Pause.)

Betty: I am pitied for my transition struggles. It's a predicament. Neither consciousness has my undivided support. Only dimly away beyond, can I see the end of the tunnel I'm in. Nevertheless I almost enjoy the pain of comprehension, because at least it is acute life. Some day I'll turn it into a harmonious existence without the struggle of contrasting conditions....

It is as if I were comfortably in calico, and somebody put ermine on me and I had to live up to it.

Here's a new idea coming along. It has had no words assigned to it. Such a big beautiful thing; I wish I could encompass it. It is terrible to have anything so big, so hopelessly nameless. I can't capture it. It is something so bright it doesn't cast any shadow. It is a borderland thing. As soon as you begin to sense it, you are a member of a different fraternity.

CHAPTER VII

BACK COUNTRY

As time went on Betty's explorations took her farther and farther into these trackless regions of the higher consciousness. I do not believe many of us can expect to duplicate them, except fleetingly and in fragment perhaps. They were, I think, special to Betty, and for special purpose; carefully guided and controlled, primarily intended as experiment and demonstration. Nor do I feel we should try to duplicate them. That would lead to disappointment and perhaps serious defeat.

Betty: Why, I can slip back and forth so easily today! It is very strange! The wind swept through me as I came in. I hailed it, did not crouch before it, and it went through me as sun goes through you. I like slipping back and forth this way. I don't see why it isn't just as interesting a performance, and vastly more desirable, than learning to swim in an element that is not your own. It is just as natural really. I just leap out of myself, and take a dive into a freer, more stimulating element. Each time I do it, it gets easier; I am more at home in it; and more stimulated by it. I am not tremendously good at it: but it's just as simple as that.

46

I am getting an actual demonstration, proof, of a spiritual existence as it is here, not in a future life. It's a very definite winged consciousness; nothing postponed or impossible of attainment about it. It's absolutely the next step we've got to take.

Now while I'm entirely possessed with it, I must try to get down to you a simple method of its acquisition. I don't want to say anything cryptic, but I must show you this way out, because this exit into greater life is the crowning glory of our existence here. It means trans-figuration into an electrified and eternal being. I've got to tell you of it by degrees, because the exit is through the doors of self.

Now stepping outside oneself actually means the practice of making one's own in imagination the condi-tions of the hour of death. I hated to say that because it throws a chill across the thing. I'll start again....

Suppose the day came for the Great Adventure of de-parting hence. Even a picnic or a vacation or a business trip demands *some* preparation. One is apt to take this tremendous step quite suddenly. What is it going to be like? Why turn our imaginations away from it so piously—or is it cowardly? Why not entertain our-selves with the buoyancy of anticipation? It is quite as speculative an amusement as contemplating a trip to Thibet, or reading what astronomers say about Mars, or any other pet flight of fancy. This has the advantage that we are actually dated up for it....

Children play beautiful games of expanding con-sciousness, supposing giants and mighty superlatives. I'm getting just such a cheerful imaginative picture of when we depart hence. It is as though everything had been taken away from me but the residue of me, such as would remain if I were to die now. It's all I've got to orient me in this new world in which I am just an embryonic being. Every circumstance of life is gone. I

47

am as unconscious of my body as ever I could possibly be. The merest shadow of its existence is on me....

It makes me feel that I personally can never be annihilated. If my body were actually taken away from me entirely, and I left in space, I feel I should continue to hold myself together, a vigorously determined entity. I might be temporarily inactive, perhaps, but I'd be convinced of my ability to participate in an existence which would be within my reach for the effort of taking. Though I might be deprived of everything en route, I could not by any conceivable thing be overcome or annihilated. I know that the development of a spark, even a tiny spark, of individual power cannot die. It will seek and find its proper progression through its own vitality. The thing to do is to take a lively spark with you when you go....

Now it seems to be an army symbol. I have assembled and set in order my possessions for the great Inspection—what it is permitted me to take along of my cherished interests. They are dominating me in the order of their ardor. I am privileged to have a preview, as it were: to consider them with growing impersonality, and reappraise them, if I so desire. That is a very illuminating process. I can go no farther until I have made satisfactory decisions of what I choose for my equipment for the journey ahead; what I will offer as confidently as possible for the great Inspector. This is the first game I play; the preliminary practice at the game of self.

I am trying to show you an actual definite possible method of controlling the first maturing, naturally and joyously, from this life to the next; occupying experimentally the higher grades, while continuing existence here. You can do this by periodically letting fall your acquiescence with the impertinences of the body and its setting of manufactured needs, its houses and parks and marts and all its complications: letting them fall deliberately from your consciousness, and at the same time being vigorously yourself; translating as into another language the same order of your ardors and pursuits. It mirrors your soul in secret to yourself....

Now I am just reposing in the entourage of vitality. I wonder if it is the actual condition of a place I am going to, or a figment of the imagination as a symbol. I can't make out; but it's real, as though I had departed into it. You see, I am away from myself entirely; I am away from all the things I like to play barnacle to....

I am going back through the gates of self now. I can see the minutiae coming into focus; the expanded things have all contracted. There merely remains greater power in the manipulation of them for the purposes decided on in my higher courts.

Betty: (After half-hour.) All the work ahead is liberation from self; my portioned-off self has become too great a restriction to me. I have found out how to blossom forth from it, but I cannot establish myself in the new atmosphere. I feel curiously like an electric attachment dragging a cord with me everywhere: I'm not free. It's a clear field, ahead, of what I've got to do; and I am working on a comprehension of it....

My experiences are like what somebody called a "tight-rope of faith." This consciousness beyond self is just the precarious elevation above what is normally ours. Equilibrium and progress rest entirely with my ability to regulate and control myself, to be sure and poised and confident and daring in a new element. I can see long practice in that ahead....

I seem to be very far out today. I can hardly see the part of me that walks below. The things people travel for—shops and sights and things—are nonexistent to me. I feel more closely akin to the smoke from the chimneys experimenting with its liberation. I am more conscious of the sweep of horizon-traveling elements from country to country, than I am of the breezes that wander down the streets.

(Long pause.)

Now I am quite successfully dead. It wasn't much of an operation after all! It was a pleasurable releasing, quite different from the death-agony idea. That should be looked on as simply the birth pains of the spiritual body.

I'm here, all right, and quite contented, but I'm like a baby that has pulled itself upright holding onto a chair: I don't know what to do next. If only I were a little stronger and more vigorous, that would put me more closely in touch with the help and affection I feel around me. Thank heaven I have the protection of it. Now I must keep still and see what my instincts and emotions are....

I seem to be only semiconscious. There is so much around me now that before I was blind and deaf to.... Oh, I strained to open what should be my earth eyes and touch with my earth fingers, and it's not possible!... Helping, loving people are around me, urging me to do something. I love them back for helping me, and it gets easier....

It is dreadful to be this way without more vitality and shape. I ought to take form right away and go at it, but I'm lumpish. I may have great possibilities and great powers, but how am I going to get hold of them? I'd like some advice about what to do. I should like to start right out and try my muscles and see what I've got, but I know I can't do that; I am not in that kind of a world....

I seem to have an impulse, some sort of an urge, to make this weakish lumpish self of mine move forward valiantly and surgingly. It's not aggression: that is a bull-headed sort of thing. It's not exactly force: that is too cold and steely a word. They are stiff-muscled words; they don't sustain the idea at all. I can't find any better than the old word "volition." I tried "faith," but that is a queer platform people put things on; it's been spoiled. So I had to go back to a suspended word that could travel vigorously.

Well, I got the volition, and I started right out, so as not to be attached to anything. I didn't want to be huddled in a corner. And I got much firmer shape right away—like being turned on a potter's wheel. Then I got something quite easily, no trouble at all. It came right away as soon as I started out: nice and warm and loving feeling. I don't know what you call it, but I'm glad I've got it. It makes me feel very slightly glowish....

Seems to me I'll have to leave myself there awhile, just brooding. I am going on with the eternal body though; I must find out how I shape it and energize it.

I've got to come back now....I'm coming like an autum leaf, zig-zag.

Betty: I must go out now. I am conscious only of careful manipulation. I feel like a tiny planetary thing cast off from a body to which I was adhering to mature. And now I am imbued with actual planetship. You remember before I was like something electrical with a cord which I dragged around to preserve my current. Now I am detached and endowed with the ability to create my own glow, my own current. I don't know how to explain how I do it; it's an instinctive thing yet. I can obtain it much as if we got electricity by radio. I am a little tiny unit of power by myself. I call it glow, because that means warmth and light both. It is a retained sensation and a radiation at the same time, which is what seems the most characteristic quality of this ideal

51

extension of myself. Strangely enough it's my real life body from now on, and I am content to have it so....

You can't beat upon a shadow and mutilate it, however clear-cut and defined it may be. You can't bottle up a sunspot and retain it for yourself. You can't mix your mediums like that. Now this is just to sweep your mind clean of its sense limitations and help you to think of yourself, your true forever self, as of an entirely different substance....

My! I'm going deep!...Still farther?...Now!

It is a direct experience of spiritual substance. I am looking at it, but am unable to comprehend it; it is so different from the skin-and-bones stuff that we have for bodies. I tell you this so you will know how puzzled I am. I've got to stay here and work in this until I understand it. When I put on a body of this I am all so changed I don't know what to do or what to tell you....

There: I've got it on! But the joke of it is that what I was doing was to get off the other one. *Now!* Here I am!...

I am just the same person, but I am entirely made of this strange new substance, which is bodiless but seems at the same time to maintain itself. It does not just dissipate with the rest of the air. I can occupy it temporarily, but I can't utilize it nor travel in it yet....

It has the most amusing possibilities. Supposing you *are* made of this: it is more like the separating and re-coagulating power of quicksilver than anything I know. If I want to go through a material thing, I just flow right through it, sieve myself through it. There is nothing *solid* you know, really. I'm so afraid of leaving some of myself behind on the other side. I am not very good at it, but I know I can. Confronted by what used to look like a solid thing like a wall, I know perfectly well I can go through it....

Supposing you took the figure of a man made up of

little dots, like a radio picture. It's a perfectly good picture; but if you separated all those dots far enough it wouldn't be. That is what astonished me so: I lost my body—freed myself from what held all the dots together—and found I was occupying the spaces, held together in some way by the spiritual body. It is very puzzling....

I can't for the life of me get used to it enough to go on. I keep trying to get the feeling of reality by crystallizing the dot figure again: I bring all the little dots together, close, tight, again; and I say, "There is what I am accustomed to seeing and being." And then I all expand, and say, "There's what I am now." Then I am made of something that was in between, of an entirely different substance—am held together only by what, long dormant and undeveloped, there was of the spirit within me when I was crystallized.

I must find out; I must intensify my differentiation, what makes me Me in my new body, instead of reverting to universal substance: I am so worried for fear I'll burst out somehow, not hold myself together. Sort of fragile, my outlines are; not strong enough to hold together well. I am awfully thin-skinned spiritually.

Betty: I am learning a great deal: this freed body of mine must be trained. I no longer get much help in actual support; I support myself. To do this I must understand the action of utilizing this freed body. I'd be afraid to explain it minutely, I am so new and ignorant and experimental. I am acting instinctively, and not intelligently....

How curious those waves are! They have a lifting quality almost supporting you, and yet they have a drawing quality that brings sustenance. How wonderful and fascinating it is! I believe there's a great princi-

53

ple there when I understand it. It's just the way a fish passes water through its gills for its sustenance. So this freed body of mine by means of this pulsation maintains itself in a higher form of ambience by passing it through itself. I am different from it and lesser than it, but I am also entirely sustained and fed by, enlivened by it. Not fed in the sense of eating, but in the sense of gaining progressive understandings.

Everything works in the same way—the pumping of hearts, systole and diastole; but it's the instant of its passing through you that is your moment of divinity, absolute unity. Thus individual life is fed. I think everything I get is the sum of these instants of unity. In time they prick out a picture, something like a wireless picture. These maintaining pulsations come entirely from the region of feeling, which we symbolize by the heart. The brain is a far member, like a hand or foot....

This pulsing business is so important. You remember the other day, when I couldn't quite function my new body? I discovered then that all I could do was just collect every bit of inner desire-power and heart-force that I possessed and fling it out of me in a great exuberant stretch. That was when I found that this pulsing action is the great life movement which you transform and adapt to produce your own individual variations. You see, it reconstructs according to what one takes into it with him of shaping desire....

One thing I want you to know: that pulsing is an *involuntary* action. You don't do it yourself; you only create a kind of yearning condition which is a suction calling it into being. You mustn't think you could pulse *yourself*, because you can't.

Betty: I get rid of my body quite easily now; like taking off a boot...Feels pretty good, but I think I've got

54

to go deeper....

I'm looking at a kind of disembodied quality, trying to understand it for you. I am on the power side, and being assisted temporarily by great force and wisdom. Under its spell I'm turning to look down to see why I don't get more of it ordinarily. It is because of the lack of this disembodied quality I am talking about. I'll get a name for it soon. We've got to incorporate it in our work.

We have all of us—our group—had a hazy conception that there are such things as higher forces that work just as well as our physical applications of force do, only superlatively. We all admit them—as weak generalizations. But still our hands and eyes and legs and ears are of far more utility to us. Now this disembodied quality I am looking at is what would give us actual possession of the working ability of these higher forces. I am up beside those who have all this to give out, and it is tremendously important to get their point of view on why we are not utilizing it. They say I can't get much of it; only a tiny beginning, a little hint on how to go about growing into it.

It is the same thing I tried to acquire the other day when my weakish lumpish body wouldn't function. I brought out all the qualities I could think of and tried them on it to make it work. Will power only gave it a sort of jerk; and concentrated energy, and all those hard tight applications, just humped it about a little, mostly in the same place. This quality is not much recognized. Actually it is just *the sureness of your belief in the existence of this greater force.* That is the principal thing to begin with.

Take an example from natural physical forces. You wouldn't have the nerve or the idiocy to try walking on water; but you step out on ice with perfect confidence. In ordinary daily living you come to associate your

55

mind so naturally and pleasurably and habitually with the great forces which control our physical universe that they grow measurably firm under the feet, as it were. Take gravitation, which always works; the magnetic attraction or the power of electricity when control is established; the buoyancy of placement in water—any of the natural laws that appeal to you. Our conscious minds approve and abandon all test of them.

But these higher forces we have sensed only as weak generalizations. We've got to make them the same in our conscious minds as the natural forces I mentioned, and which we accept as a matter of course. We've got to associate with them, experiment with them, as constantly and interestedly as people did in acquiring the laws controlling the other forces. It's the thing that will make our spiritual bodies work. It's the first thing we shall be faced with when we "go hence." Everything we have been accustomed to will have gone away from us. If we haven't built this extension of confidence in known forces, we will be at a loss. This particular attitude of mind, surety, confidence is *itself* a force: it *is* a superlative force.

Invisible: What we are stepping around is to avoid the use of the word "faith." We don't want to use it until we have freshened it. It's been made respectable by calling it suggestion: you all know the power of that. Only this is its simon-pure reality, its *essence*.

(Pause.)

Betty: They told me I couldn't get much of it, only enough to begin acquiring this force. I'll tell you how I'm doing it.

I made a sort of cradle of confidence of the tides and the moons and the planetary swings; and I said, there's no reason why I shouldn't rest this spirit of me securely in these unfailing forces. I felt delightfully in suspension, restful with everlasting-arms restfulness. This extension of my personality, the reality I call myself, by my name, has quite reasonably ventured out to associate with unseen but thoroughly tested realities. That's the beginning: that is how we begin to grow into the higher forces.

I have a funny way of working. I vary all kinds of tests. I jump up and down on natural laws to feel their reality. Mentally I turn and twist them all, and jiggle them around, and they still hold me up with a sureness of cause and effect.

Now I will leave that side for a minute and seek the society of the greater forces.

Invisible: You see, we've brought you forth from your lesser self to your greater self.

(Long pause.)

Betty: Feels sort of like a blind person walking along. I feel when I get in a sunspot of power, and I try to keep in it, and when I stray out of it I try to get back. I know it's there, and I just have to make my senses so acute that I can keep in it or get back to it if I stray.

Each person must play his own mental game in this thing. I am only suggesting mine....

All this is an effort to establish us firmly in the spiritual so we can utilize its greater powers in doing the physical things we see are worth doing. This definite belief in a force assisting our best efforts, and our reckoning on its unfailing help; the establishment of this principle of the constructive, directive forward movement which we call evolution—this condition of faith, must at some time or other in our progression be permanently accepted by our united being. It is a magic touchstone, making positive our efforts, instead of negativing them constantly with doubts and waverings.

There is only one important proviso: we cannot depend on this law to accomplish anything more than

57

the *complement* of our own efforts. One must depend on oneself to build one's aspirational column, knowing that at the highest stretch of one's hopes and efforts a capital will be placed beyond one's power to conceive.

Life! life! life! Life is so fascinating! I pursue it as it chuckles into every shape. Fast in my faith I can follow my devious route, because I know the source, and can return to it, and excavate my little bits of truth. Life, life, life! I want to live it! But you can't live it happily and humorously and powerfully until you are first made fast in faith and perception with reality. I feel eager and loving towards life, it's a beautiful pattern, but I haven't stuff enough in me to cover it. I want more stuff in me to cover it. Everything that touches my senses must make me more porous to it. Sea-breathing things, underwater things, air and earth-breathing things; the very sun motes; the very shadows between the stars speak eloquently, each according to its kind, in the great pageant of life. I don't want to be a scholar, or a courtier, or a soldier, or anything else like that in the pageant. I want to wear motley. I want to be the Fool, and so come close to all kinds. I want to receive and give back the truth in the fertile form of lighthearted jest. I want to live in this fluid, flexible condition, because it is happy and easily disseminates.

CHAPTER VIII

THE LAY OF THE LAND

Though the Invisibles had the definite purpose of leading us into higher consciousness, they did not continuously keep us tiptoe. They seemed to be very wise people, and they understood well the necessity of occasional breathing times in less rarified air. And they set their faces always against any attitude, at any time, of hushed and reverent solemnity. It was, in the beginning, difficult for us bystanders to keep from being portentous. We were impressed by the importance of what was being given; and we had not learned to distinguish between importance and solemnity. Theirs is a laughing philosophy. They agreed with Stevenson, who said

59

of religion, "If it makes you gloomy, depend upon it, it is wrong." They did not fear to be funny; to "josh" at times; to crack jokes with us; and it seemed to me that they got as much relish out of these interludes as we did ourselves. At the very first some of us, through old habit of mind, were instinctively abashed, as though someone had laughed aloud in church. Why shouldn't one laugh aloud in church? they asked reasonably.

"This subject," said they, "is light-footed; not like the solemn tread of a processional. It has dance steps in it, and running for the joy of running, and leaping for the joy of leaping. It is as natural and cheerful as a baby playing with its toes, feeling out the most desirable activity for entertainment. This is a *gracious* performance. It is not a child in a schoolroom; it is a soul gracefully entering into eternity."

"They are terribly anxious," added Betty, "to take away any solemn ecclesiastical idea from 'spiritual.' Once recognized as standing for spontaneous enjoyment, legitimate heart indulgence, the word will have rough-and-ready hiking clothes instead of vestments."

Betty fell naturally into this lightheartedness. She was always kicking up her heels in frivolity; a tendency we at first deplored. We were always trying to herd her back to what we considered the serious job, but were invariably laughed at for our trouble. Sometimes, indeed, the Invisibles announced a "party," and for a whole evening regaled us with stories and doggerel, verse and small talk. After a while we managed to loosen up and enjoy heartily these occasions. We called them "sag back parties," and recognized them as necessary breathing spaces.

In these breathing spaces we found occasional indulgences for our curiosity. We were always full of questions about all sorts of things that interested us, but which had little or nothing to do with the case. I can see now that we must have been most annoying, for these people had a definite plan, and such questions only got in the way of it. What was life like over there? What should we do in this or that situation? What might be the Cosmic Plan in regard to this or that?

Generally they sidetracked us, but in the long run we did manage to sneak in a considerable body of statement. Too great a body to quote in full here. They no more fit with our present purpose than they fitted into the Invisibles' main plan. But a few of them may serve to the reader, as they did to us, as breathing spaces.

Some of our questions seemed to us *very* important. What sort of people are we going to be when we "go hence"? A friend who was sitting in with us was much exercised over that. He wanted something solid and definite to tie to. Contact with wraiths did not seem much fun to him. At first the Invisibles hesitated to answer. Their conditions were so different, and mistranslation had so often resulted in things repellent to common sense.*

Invisible: When you think of us don't bother about our shape or substance. It is a living and loving form still: nothing unnatural or vaporous. Don't make such an unattractive picture of the change. Keep us in your hearts as we were; it is nearer the truth, and more comforting than trying to comprehend the difference. The more naturally you can think about us, the less apt you are to go astray on phantoms of your own conception. Dear me, why *do* you get so *fantastic* over that? It's terrible to be loved so fleshlessly! It handicaps a con-

---

* Such as the unfortunate "cigars" in Sir Oliver Lodge's *Raymond*.

ception of warmth and response existing *as*-ever and *for*-ever.

Betty: They're so real, so real, and so much more vibrant. It is a pity; isn't it?...If you'd only try to say just what you are we wouldn't make such silly mistakes....

Oh! I'm getting a little more of things as they're going to be over there....Wait; I want to look at them....

Each person is endowed with force, individual progressive force. That's the main difference. It lifts the whole mass into a different freer state, clear and bright, devoid of *weight!* It's mostly the feeling of power and lightness. So vital, light and strong, that life!

I wish I could stay with you and get that way too! You're made out of—I don't know—so much clearer, thinner, stronger stuff!...

I'm going; but I know now what you are like.

Stewart: Try to tell me before you come out.

Betty: It is no different in form; it's a difference of element, more especially of clearness and light and power; without the thick clumsy dragging substance we are in. It is a much greater difference of element than going under water. We haven't any similar contrast. I feel people of different substance, but *entire*. They are not distinct to me. Their body walls are thinner than our body walls; more akin to the substance they are in, so they are more susceptible to it in getting their energy out of it. (Long pause.)

Connecting link I don't get. How do we...I must think about this. When do we most nearly approximate that state? That's the point to work out.

Invisible: Great energy and force put into living raises the entire being above the control of the physical. There have been many demonstrations of this in times of great emotional stimulation or necessity of action.

Now compare yourself with lower physical forms of

greater density. Gradually, loosening of density produces finer, lighter form beings in the region of consciousness. Indefinitely extended, it reaches to the condition just manifested.

Stewart: I don't want to quibble about words, but I do want to understand how literal they are. I am much higher in perception than a mud turtle; but my actual flesh, as flesh, is not as tender as his.

Invisible: Man's physical organism is vastly more refined, sensitive, less dense than that of the turtle. Density is the difference in *reaction quality*.

Fair enough, said our friend, I think I could get along with that sort of a fellow. But how about any real individual relationships, such as we know them? How about our mates? And if we haven't found them here, do we find them there? Or is there such a thing as eternal bachelorhood?

Invisible: No, most decidedly not. They quickly find their complementary selves. They then unite for greater harmony of effort and complete happiness.

Stewart: Between those thus mated is there any form of what might be called private relationship; that is, a relationship peculiar to them as individuals, corresponding, however vaguely, to our physical relationships?

Invisible: Your world is full of the ecstacy of harmonious attraction, beginning at the mere chemical affinities and proceeding upward to the sex relations. This same magnetic attraction continues, but in vastly higher and even more ecstatic form. It takes place eventually through perfect union of complementary spiritual halves. It is a little difficult to put concisely, as there are many ramifications and half-realized conditions before the perfect mating takes place. That is not very satisfactory as an explanation, but you may rest assured that the beauty of physical mating is not lost, but intensively increased in the spiritual realm.

Stewart: Mated relations here have two phases or angles: the fairly uniform affectional relation, and the occasional intensified relation. Do both exist there in any form?

Invisible: Discouragingly complex subject, because all affection is infinitely varied in all stages of acquisition. We cannot take you into conditions beyond your human imagination. We can only vaguely satisfy with what will be your next step.

It is rather more crescendo than spasmodic. Just as on earth you rise to certain heights by occasional bliss, so here by harmony you obtain these heights. Perhaps occasionally you have them dimmed by periods of distraction, but the heights are always there, and obtainable and extendible. In time you can grow permanently into your highest ideal and remain there, the while you occasionally scale even greater heights. This is progressive bliss, intensified as you grow into greater capabilities of realization.

Stewart: All of which is a property of the two, mated, of opposite sex; as opposed to being a common relation of all spirits?

Invisibles: Yes. But with your present earth ideas and desires, you cannot fully appreciate how change of structure will influence your ideas. Don't you see, we are trying to tell you that we do have something private between just the two, but change of structure and wider vision change your desire for so intensely personal an attitude. It is absolutely possible. Only as the child cannot comprehend the grown-up ideal, so you cannot now put your earth desires as a standard for what you will desire when you get here.

These fragments are typical of the way we learned the lay of the land. They are valuable not so much as statements of fact as flashes that reveal glimpses beyond our ordinary experiences. We shall have an adjustment to make; but it will be a natural and easy adjustment. A lot of our customary standards are to be jettisoned. They will be as out of place as a buggy whip in a motor car. Take space, by which we measure so much of ourselves.

Betty: I see; space is only an imaginary boundary, not a definite reality. How curious it looks! There isn't any such thing as that word-pattern we call space. It's altogether different!...

This is too much for me! My goodness! There's no use trying to figure it out while you're living. You couldn't hold onto the idea when you brought it back! I don't believe I could *stand* an idea like that and get back and live again sensibly. But I'll try to tell you. I'm gasping over it, and I'll spoil it; but I'll try....

Yesterday when I looked at a pebble under the microscope, I looked down into a deep canyon of space. How can you measure space? How can you give anything so elastic and changing the name of space? I can walk on that pebble; and yet, by the magic of concentration, a tiny crevice in it can be refracted to the illusion of a real canyon with true immensity. Don't you see, space is not real at all. It is contained in an attribute of your consciousness.

Invisible: Consider the magnitude of your own illusion of space as compared with a pebble. Now raise it again to an incomprehensible magnitude such as you can only guess at.

Betty: We are all apparently occupying the same space. It doesn't seem to be a case of distance at all. This is quite new to me and very satisfactory; because I never could see how they'd have room for everything

65

and everybody who'd ever died. This is much better; only I can't understand it clearly....

Well, anyhow, I'm never going to have any respect for space again, because I know now it's altogether too unreliable. It depends utterly on who is looking at it. I'm sorry I did not get that intelligently, but anyway it was a grand muckraking and exposure of space! You see, it's a word that hasn't any standing at all, except with us. It represents only what *we* think about it. But I must say it's rather exhausting to struggle with, since I don't seem to have much influence with it, and have work to do in it!

Invisible: Space is not distance: space is degrees of perception. Distance is only slowness in getting there.

All progress leads from the more material to the less material; until at length it conducts us into regions where reality is perceived without the use of any laborious material structure at all. You yourselves know that individuals of higher mentality do not always have to pass through a material experience. If they are cognizant of its cause and effect, they can grasp it without painstakingly suffering it: they do not need the laborious material structure to see its reality. It is the same way in the still higher levels beyond. You are all leading up to a consciousness of reality without its material shadows, its material reflections, its material manifestations, as aids to comprehension.

CHAPTER IX

PORTAGE

The foregoing may give a rough idea of what was given Betty for her own development, and by way of evidence as to the nature of the higher consciousness into which she was being led. My own function during this period was largely as reporter; but in due course I also had my innings. Part of the plan seemed to be some form of publication; and my profession pointed to me as the one to do the actual writing.

Now as a writer I have never been able to do effective work at second hand. For me there is little carrying power in anything written from the outside. Tourist impressions are never more than amusing. I have never been able to go out deliberately for local color. I have had to work at the job in the lumber camps; ride the Arizona ranges after cattle; pot round the back of beyond in old-time Africa or Alaska or wherever, doing whatever the inhabitants have to do, without ulterior motive, because I liked it, and for no other reason. Then, after it was all lived through,

I would find I had something to write about.

It was exactly so here.

If I was to do this writing job, I must do something beside report; I must myself actually live the life of the country.

Up to this point, in spite of so much admonition to the contrary, I had clung to my intellect as my best guide. I *understood* the directions given in *The Betty Book*, and subsequently, I admitted their logical truth. As ideas they were satisfactory. Also my esthetic sense found them beautiful. But now, abruptly, I found I was no longer after ideas. I was after something back of ideas—something that could no longer be a subject of thought.

Aroused and disturbed, I realized that if I wanted to get any farther I must begin to follow directions—and that I must start from the beginning. I had accompanied Betty such a long way, mentally, that I had a lot of practical back-tracking to do.

What was the very first step? On reflection I found only one thing of which I felt absolutely sure: my aim. I wanted to get into this new region of consciousness which Betty had been describing. That much was clear. Also, on further reflection, it dawned on me that the first thing I must do, if I wanted to go somewhere else, was to learn how to get away from where I was.

For the first time, I think, I understood why so many doctrines, particularly those of the Orient, insist on exercises in "getting out of the body." My practical Western mind had long balked at this concept. The image, to me, was of some sort of astral vehicle floating about, like a captive balloon, in some sort of beatific— but dense—psychic fog. It had given me a good laugh, but had failed to convince me.

Recently, however, I had had to change my mind about this. Betty certainly was getting away from her workaday vehicle into an environment that contained things not perceptible to ordinary bodily senses. Any doubt of this had finally collapsed under her repeated demonstrations that she could even travel some thousands of very earthly miles and look in on the doings of friends. That she was there, somehow, she had proved beyond doubt by reporting to me all sorts of details—who was there and what they were doing at a particular time—and these details had subsequently been checked, as accurate, by correspondence. On these occasions, *some* part of her consciousness was indubitably "out of her body"; for her body, blindfolded, was all the while next my hand. Furthermore the "she-herself," the perceptive part that could observe and remember and comment, had accompanied that traveling portion of consciousness. It was aware of events in Boston; it was unaware—or only dimly aware—for the time being of Burlingame, California.

Faced with this evidence, my cautious skepticism retired a pace or two, but quickly took refuge in another defense. Betty and these other people, I argued, were different. They were gifted; they were "psychic." It was all very well for them. But I did not consider myself "psychic." I was just an ordinary person, like everyone else. This "getting out of the body" business was beyond me; and if it had to be done before I could go ahead, why then I—and the ordinary run of people like me—was just out of luck.

I did not then appreciate that "psychic" is just a word: that everyone is "psychic," just as everyone is alive; that anyone can "get outside the body" any time he wants to; that in fact we are all doing this, to a degree, every day of our lives.

"We have a house with five doors," Betty explained.

69

"There are others, but they are secret doors. The five doors are your senses. What do you suppose your senses were given you for, besides to keep you from falling down? Don't you see?—it's so soft and nice; it sounds so wonderful; it smells so good; it looks so fair; I've got a hunger for it. Now where's my body? You are 'in your body' only when you shut all the doors one after the other, and huddle down within it. Then you get a cramp in it, get poisoned air in it, get stiff and stupid in it!

"So if you want the secret of life, of how to live beyond your ken, you will start in practicing. You will do it in foolish fashions, too. You will pat good things. You will smell good things. And every time you do it, you will cry: There is a way out!

"The senses are so like wings of the spirit that I am making a beautiful design for the Doorway of the Senses. They would be great wings, crossed a little at the top, showing the pearly opalescence beyond. I will make a *beautiful* Doorway of the Senses!"

This was a marvelous revelation to me, somewhat analagous to M. Jourdain's world-shaking discovery that all along he had been talking prose. It seemed too obvious to be true. Nevertheless, when I turned it over carefully in my mind, it seemed to withstand the test of logic. There was no doubt about it: every time I stopped my usual busy concern with what was going on inside my head to look upon the physical world—by this slight gesture I was undoubtedly transferring a portion of my consciousness outside the limits of my compact self. This minute I was inside myself, thinking my busy thoughts, making my plans, concerning myself with my symptoms, or just buzzing around idly in a too-usual aimless fashion. Of anything outside myself I was just sufficiently cognizant to keep from bumping into it. The next minute I had moved outside myself to

70

companionship with the trees and birds and flowers and clouds and sky lines, deserting my usual preoccupations within.

"Getting outside the body," then, in its first simple beginning at least, was not so mysterious and occult a performance as the words implied. It was simply a matter of attention. If I transferred my attention from within myself to outside myself, my consciousness followed. I had the method. It remained only to apply it to this other field of activity.

Before continuing with what is to be said about "getting out of the body," one thing must be made clear. This process is nothing desirable in itself. The body is no stepchild. In final analysis it is full partner, and neglect of it, or ignoring of it, may be as disasterous to the whole entity as subservience to it. Anything acquired from the spiritual, anything whatever, must ultimately be brought to the physical and amalgamated with it, before the process is complete.

In my own case I was soon made to see that this getting aside from the body was intended only as a temporary freeing from its demands in order that I might act untrammeled in another part of myself: and also, as a by-product, that I might actually experience, by sensation, that the body is only an attribute of the spirit. Like the mind. As are the hands to the body itself.

I emphasize this point here because a great many people, "psychically inclined," seem to think they are accomplishing a deed of merit when they manage to "get out of the body." It is not meritorious: It is dangerous, if done for and by itself.

71

Unfortunately the application of the method turned out to be harder than it looked. In order to transfer my attention from within myself, I discovered I must provide it with some sort of a definite landing place. I couldn't just transfer it to nothing at all. Imagination plus Betty's descriptions of my objective helped some, but the results remained thin and unconvincing at best. The trouble was, I finally decided, that I did not have the *feel* of what I was after. To be sure I'd had a few small, sporadic "psychic" experiences, as has about everybody else. But these had really been just amusing external stunts. Nothing had ever happened "inside," in the sense of inner visions, or "spiritual" sensations or perceptions. At least nothing I could identify as such—and certainly nothing I could use as a definite target.

Then one day, unexpectedly, the Invisibles took a hand.

"There are people around me," it was Betty speaking, "lots of people; a nice human crowd. There seems to be a message for you; but I can't get it—something nice: a recognition that is coming to you...."

"We come today," broke in the Invisible, "to blend our spirits with yours and make you feel the great heart expansion. Put down the pencil, close your eyes, and just give way to the change. Open up and welcome it."

I did as I was told, and at once experienced a most peculiar "balloony" sensation, as though I were being rapidly expanded in every direction. This was almost immediately succeeded by a curious inner effect most difficult to describe. It was very similar to the sensation of bodily relaxation, only it seemed rather to be a relaxation and expansion of the normally tight compactness of the gathered-in mind. In my notes of the occasion I find the words, "Impossible to convey, but a very definite and unexpected phenomenon." In-

72

stantly, sharply, I understood why the Invisibles had refused to try to explain a lot of things to me in words; the words just wouldn't have made sense to me. How would you, for instance, convey any adequate idea of sight to a person born blind?

The experience continued for quite an extended interval, during which I remained fully conscious and watchful, but withdrawn, as it were, into a kind of cleared space in the center of my consciousness. Then gradually I emerged and became cognizant of my surroundings once more.

"We have tried today," said the Invisible, "to teach you the sensation which is the symptom of expanding life, to demonstrate for your recognition the actual feeling of it. For the present we ask only that you seek this sensation, partake of it, and acquire a hunger for it. It is the reality of which we have talked in discussing the association with the spirit. Forget the words and get the reality. Establish yourself in it, naturally, simply, without great effort, as you would sit in the sun and rejoice in its warmth.

"We leave today before the wane," concluded the Invisible. "We wish to preserve at its height the impression of the blending of the two elements."

The very next day I was instructed to continue my experiment.

"Don't be expectant," warned the Invisible. "Be flexible. Also don't write. You must get complete control of physical relaxation."

After a short pause I felt again the balloony sensation, and immediately after, an indescribable impression of rapid vibration. This in turn was succeeded by a combined floating and expanding feeling of great power. It lasted for only a few moments, and then ebbed away.

"Rest a moment," instructed the Invisible. "Relax. Think of anything you desire."

"It seems to me," said I, "that my voluntary muscles are entirely relaxed. What beyond that?"

"It's not so much physical muscles," said the Invisible, "as mental adhesions which prevent detachment long enough at a time to establish security in the new sensation. For the present just try to break up these adhesions. They are difficult for us to control. We lift you, transmute you; but there is a drag. Now put down your pencil and try again, without expectancy, but with outgoing response."

For perhaps ten seconds the sense of vibration and expansion proceeded much as before. Then, quite without warning, a band of white light seemed suddenly to be drawn across my eyes, much like a bandage. This was not exactly a brilliant light, though it was quite luminous; it was more like a ground-glass light than anything I can think of. Gradually it gained in depth and took on color, until it had changed itself into a veil of singularly lucent ultramarine blue. At the same time the sense of expansion and vibration heightened measurably. Then quite rapidly the whole thing ebbed away, and I found myself in my chair once more.

"They were all around you," said Betty, "as though they were lifting you. But it was more like a stretching exercise. Very curious: a stretching of the spirit."

"If you could once," added the Invisible, "feel secure and natural in this higher element, you could enter it at will. Meanwhile learn to experiment with the relaxing qualities of it; gain merely the technique of occasionally freeing yourself."

"What were those light and color effects?" I asked. "Are they retinal, or are they something to do with this other element?"

"They are a symptom," said the Invisible. "Your

own control and power to take is still weak, because confidence is not yet established. Therefore we search for a method of bringing it to you more palpably. Any physical stepping stone makes this process more easily handled and tangible. Somehow you must establish confidence in your ability to isolate yourself in an entirely different and superior element.

"This is not easy to attain; never is. Your desire is to keep it reduced to the element you are used to; our desire is to free you from that restricted comprehension and force you to come to a higher one. You want to translate back everything we give; we also want you to go ahead and write it—provided you experience it more frequently in the original. But remember one thing: it cannot fail to be anything but vague and impractical and intangible, if you persist in centering your interest on the translation. Explore first; write about it afterwards."

The third experience of this nature—and the last for some time—took place a few days later. It was in a sense a continuation and extension of the previous experiences. The vibratory sensations began again with great power. But now they seemed to begin in some remote inner depths, and expand constantly outward, carrying my consciousness with them. The final result was an utterly novel sensation of awareness diffused most curiously beyond the centered kernel of ordinary life.

The visual "symptoms" also were repeated. The band of white light appeared as before, gradually changed to ultramarine that gathered in patches, slowly collected to a common center, contracted into a pin point and disappeared, only to be succeeded by others. It was as though I looked into a strange and gorgeous kaleidoscope. At the last the color deepened to a rich purple. I may add that I tried several times experimentally to induce these color effects by myself. Such efforts were uniformly unsuccessful.

The entire experience may have lasted a minute or two—not more. Then I was once again at my table, the words of the Invisibles sounding in my ears.

"All we have tried to do," said they, "was to impart directly to you the sensation of the reality of spiritual substance. We wanted to give you a feeling of confidence in it as a real world. This contact is what you need most at present. In time it will not be difficult for you to get merely the sensation; and full realization is not necessary in order to work in it.

"There is no satisfactory explanation of it that we can give you as yet. For a while we prefer to leave it to experience. Retain the memory of the *sensation*. Fix it firmly for a future point of departure. After experiencing it a few times, it will be no longer merely a series of strange sensations, but a reality to be returned to with confidence."

At this point another warning must be emphasized. The reader must not sit down in any attempt to reproduce the details of my own experience. Nor must he gauge his success or failure by the presence or absence of the "balloony feeling," the band of light, or any of the other symptoms I have described. For that is just what they are—symptoms, and personal symptoms at that. They are by-products, not ends in themselves; and any attempt to make an end of a by-product is likely to result in disaster.

Naturally some sort of symptoms will accompany any accomplishment. They will occur, spontaneously, to everyone healthfully reaching toward the higher con-

76

sciousness. But never, never are they to be consciously pursued as a definite objective—or even anticipated in the exact form encountered by someone else.

In recent years I have talked with a great number of people making this journey, and have swapped yarns with them of our experiences. Generally, sooner or later, our trails have converged. But the early details are often so astonishingly different that one might be tempted to believe we had different objectives. This fact we must face, and understand. The country we are entering is a vast region of infinite variety, and if we insist on searching fixedly for some particular detail of topography, we may nose about shortsightedly as a mole until we manage to get ourselves into very dangerous territory.

Indeed so ephemeral is the importance of the symptoms themselves that I found, in my own case, they disappeared soon after their function had been fulfilled. I soon abandoned any attempt to recapture them, even as expedients toward reaching the state of higher consciousness described. I was not instructed to do this in so many words, but some intuition warned me that lights and colors and such were not what I was after. Even the "balloony" feeling and the sensation of expanding consciousness, I quickly realized, were only crude, almost physical, symbols. The thing itself was a kind of *essence* of these things, a subtle and profound inner state impossible to describe. It was this that I eventually learned to practice and to trust.

Why, then, it is fair to ask, have I quoted in such detail those symptoms of my own experience? Merely because I hope they may be reassuring to the average individual interested in this exploration. Most beginners, if my own early reactions are any criterion, feel the need of a concrete relationship, through their own senses and subjective feeling. They acknowledge this higher consciousness business as desirable, but hope-lessly vague. It has too little tangible solidity. It is, to one leading a three-dimensional existence, altogether too unsubstantial. It needs reality, and vitality. It just hasn't any corners to it.

As a matter of fact, however, it is entirely substan-tial. When one finally steps over into this new country, there is no guess-work about it—nothing nebulous or indefinite. He *knows* it.

And he *knows* that he hasn't just made up the whole thing. A great many interested people have faced me with just this point. I am a writer of fiction, accus-tomed to imagining things. I know the difference.

I suppose the experiences I have just described were, in a minor way, what is called an illumination. At least the results, within myself, were important enough to justify that designation. Up to now I had gained, largely from Betty's descriptions, at least a foggy *idea* of what the higher consciousness was like. In a general way, perhaps, I *understood* what I wanted. But as an idea, and an understanding; it had been a matter only of the brain and the intellect. Now, however feebly and frag-mentarily, I had touched an underlying reality. A cold and detached idea had been replaced by an intimate sen-sation which I felt was an actual part of my own sub-stance. And as a result, I no longer needed the kind of faith described by the small boy as ''believin' in things you know ain't so.''

In this I do not fancy myself as exceptional or specially favoured. The form my own experiences took may—or may not—have been more or less peculiar to me: but some such experience, I am convinced, always goes with arrival at a certain stage of the journey. It is an essential of each person's progress.

"For true illumination," said the Invisibles, "one must attain, not only intellectual conviction, but emotional conviction; not only the perception of the satisfied equation, but also the cosmic satisfaction which has nothing to do with the pure mathematics of the intellect. An intellectual conviction gained through study, through the reading of books, through the experimental examination of evidence, has one function and one function only; it moves the center of interest into the path in which personal experience is most likely to be encountered.

"Furthermore, it will be found that when each individual has reached that point of inner growth where he is ready to contain the emotional conviction, the experience personal to himself never lacks. He may not anticipate its coming or even seek it: generally in our own lives we fail to see the sure action of evolution taking place—fail to see the same maturing as takes place in a chestnut burr. This clings tight in one undivided sealed ball until the proper moment to split on definitely prepared lines, to turn back and eject the product of its heart. Likewise the moment comes inevitably for the culmination of our efforts, whether consciously or unconsciously those efforts have been directed or misdirected. And at that moment the experience appropriate to the individual always is supplied. It is inexorable.

"In support of what I say, you will find, if you but inquire deeply enough, that each man who has within himself a true and living conviction can trace its beginning to some personal psychic experience, however small. That is part of our work; and that is in general a true test that we can apply, a sure means of evaluating the degree to which a person's spiritual consciousness has advanced. It is like one drop of a chemical which, by turning to visible color the contents of a vessel,

79

makes evident how much of another chemical is there already in suspension. If a second vessel be so treated, but containing none of the chemical, no effect will be produced. Some of us,* influenced perhaps by affection, perhaps by inexperience, apply such a test prematurely and therefore without result. How many people will you find who at one time or another have had what they call a 'queer experience'?

"This principle of ripeness must be applied in all teaching. Therefore it is not our present object to convince the world in general of anything except the need for continued conscious spiritual growth. The conviction of one thing or another will come naturally and easily and inevitably to each individual when he rises by his own specific gravity to that point. It will come to the world only when the common consciousness by its own specific gravity has also risen to that point."

---

* I.e., the Invisibles.

It's about the ripening of life. She says the fruition of life is tremendously beautiful, if it is only understood and looked at. She is showing me many things with that idea in them, but nobody is helping me with words....

It is, roughly speaking, about what we miss by keeping the greenness of youth as a standard, instead of the natural fulfillment of life, which matures like a seed pod and renews itself. The seed-renewal idea is really younger than the greenness of youth, if it is really the vitality of newness we want.

CHAPTER X

THE GREAT ADVENTURE

When we speak of "illumination," ordinarily, we have the idea of something extra-special, reserved for a favored few as a direct revelation from God. There are such. But the general fact of illumination is much homelier, and in it we all have a share; we all experience it, and fairly often. If we wished to rename this we might call it the customary complement that comes at a point of ripeness—any point of ripeness. And that again may be re-expressed in a single word—maturity.

Maturity is a culmination of points of ripeness. Throughout the formative years we accumulate, grow into, the various scattered elements of life. Then one day, quite suddenly, things click into place. We may have little understanding, intellectually, of what has happened. But we are aware of a new-found poise, a stable placement in life. We have had an illumination, we have reached the maturity appropriate to our place in evolution.

Fortunately maturity is a variable. It is not a fixed point, but moves up as the race moves up. In the Stone Age maturity was no higher than the physical. The

81

Neanderthal succumbed at twenty-six from a crack on the head because advancing years had deprived him of the zip and agility he had commanded at twenty. If by good luck he managed for a while to dodge that kind of trouble, he had really nothing to look forward to but mere existence. That was all there was in life—physical prowess. It was to be a long time before cunning and craft and wisdom were to make later life worth anything; win the old man a little sufferance from others—and from himself. And even in that there was more backward-looking in regrets than present satisfaction.

We have come a long way from primitive man—in some respects. But not in others. Many of the old cavedays standards still linger as sort of vestigial remains. Without realizing it, most of us pay disproportionate tribute to the capacities of the body. We are still holding fast to the idea of physical energy as a symbol of the pinnacle of life. In a kind of arrested development we stick at the same point as Neanderthal man, glorying in his bodily exuberances. For even today, certainly, the old man who acts in forward-looking vigor is numbered perhaps by hundreds as against untold millions living in wistfulness of vanished youth. The average man, meanwhile, is engaged in expending the accumulations made at the peak of youth, spreading them thin over the years, until at last he stands bankrupt before his gray remaining days, searching half-heartedly for some interest real enough to carry him through.

It is a sad fact, but we are still clinging to youth-worship, the Neanderthal man's superstition of youth. His instinct that youth is irreplaceable. The fallacy that at its envanishment with the rose, life's sweet-scented manuscript *does* close! We argue otherwise to ourselves. We recoil with humorous dismay from the idea of being twenty again. But the instinct persists.

There is in store for us, however, a second major

ripening, a kind of second maturity. And one of our illuminations at this time is the recognition of the youth-cult as a Neanderthal superstition.

For those beyond the half way mark who have felt this drag of the backward glance, the Invisibles had a certain gentle derision.

"Imagine," said they, "an acorn just *devastated* with grief because it had cracked its shell in putting forth its first sprout toward being an oak tree! *Its* onward-pressing conviction, maintaining the movement of life, leaves no regret for the fulfilled natural processes. Likewise with yourselves, mere accustomedness and sentiment must not retard and weaken the force of continuity. Youth welcomes every change; so should age! Age with imagination, age with freedom to forevision unhampered by the metamorphosis of a completing cycle!

"Such an outlook is not too difficult, provided you use a little understanding. Consider the bright ardor of living, the fervid desires that you have in youth. They are possible principally because of the flexibility of the physical mechanism. The secret of this golden age is the freedom from bodily restraints. The leap of the flame is the natural process. In later life you strive to recapture this faculty. But, though the *ideals* you envision have now more substance than ever before, you cannot levitate and vitalize them. Every effort to do so merely stiffens and exhausts the body machine.

"The trouble is that you are trying to translate the ardor and fervor of the intangible substance of thought into terms of bodily tensions. That is a very great mistake. If you are going to face a great and shining future, you must use a new and bright apparatus with which to express your greater capacities. You can't think bright and shining thoughts with a tired old brain. So step aside from it, admitting that it is perhaps a little of everything you say. Why shouldn't it be, and what of it? It is only a protective covering now for the thing that counts, which is what generates your bright and shining thoughts—the new consciousness born within you.

"It is a sort of replacement idea. Once you grasp it clearly you will find you have within you a fountain of eternal youth. But it must be done *honestly*. You cannot come into possession of it if you hang onto old crowbait ideas of leaning on a stick and being weighty. The instant you find yourself leaning heavily on the waning powers of the body, snatch yourself away from it. Actually, it is a clumsy, moldy, wasteful idea; and the replacement idea is the truth. After all, why saturate your whole being with a sensation that has to do with only a smaller part of it? Even when the body *is* tired, there is no longer any need for *you* to live in its tiredness. Just take the sensible measures appropriate to a tired body, and then withdraw into your higher serenities.

"Of course, it would be silly to deny that you have lost what the college boys possess. But it would be equally silly for you to think in terms of this merely physical desirability, for you are engaged in growing something younger and better than they have. This thing you are ripening toward is the fruit of your life. It will make you bright inside, no matter what you are outside. It is a *shining* thing."

"We must teach ourselves to recognize it," Betty contributed. "It is there, awaiting our recognition, for our enjoyment and development. It is the fruit of consciousness which the college boys haven't got. As soon as we let drop from it the tired flesh-thoughts, we'll see how beautiful and buoyant and wonderful it is. But as long as we allow those old flesh-thoughts to sit around like old black crows, just spoiling the party, we'll never

84

be able to believe in the fruit of our life. It will be obscured by the age of our arteries, denied by the stiffness of our muscles and every other old kill-joy in our bodies...."

"The gift of illumination of the moment," resumed the Invisibles, "is how to substitute for bodily functions the higher intelligence and vital intensities of the enduring being within you. Age, in a sense, is self-inflicted, a legacy from past generations. But within each there is something that is superior to age. Once you fully realize this, there will be no tradition of age to uphold. It will exist only as a physical cycle, quite apart from the real center of being.

"And with this realization will come another: that you are *not* on the down-slope toward bankruptcy of youth's qualities when youth itself is over—that there is something even better to look forward to: something with increasing instead of diminishing interest, and not merely limited to itself, but with vistas far into the future."

Another vestigial Neanderthal point of view is our attitude toward death. Even to those of us who believe that life goes on after death, our passing out of earth life looks like a pretty stiff bump, a sharp dividing line in continuity. If it were indeed such, its discussion could hardly be appropriate to such teachings as these, for they purport to deal with living, not dying.

But the Invisibles do not see it that way. There is no bump, no jar. We keep right on, just as we have been going. How is that? Why, said they, look at what you *have* been doing. You started out completely identified in consciousness with your physical body. As a baby you were hardly aware of any outside world. Your growth has been a steady progress away from that identification. You have become increasingly aware of the outside world. You have even come to the point where, to a degree, you have ceased to think of your body as yourself. It is more like a useful machine. You have seen how, just by noticing things, paying real attention to them, your consciousness has left its body behind to a certain and ever increasing extent. The norm of growth is to make that transfer oftener and more complete. You "develop outside interests." In the due course of events there comes a time when you find it handier and more comfortable to move your headquarters out to those outside interests. You shut up the old house, and move into a new habitation that is closer to your work. That is death.

And, they added, get over any idea that death is going instantaneously to transfigure you into Celestial Beings. You did not leap to maturity when you graduated from high school into college.

"There is no sudden jump," they insisted, "which will transform you. You take over what you are. That is the real continuity. It's not the continuity of going over to something easier and adapted to all your peculiarities. It is a smooth transition. You might just as well accept it. You've got to do away with that superstition that your handicaps here will be instantly eliminated there. Get adapted here, and then you will enter without conditions. It's a smooth beautiful thing, this continuity. The division between the lives is an imaginary line, like the equator."

It follows logically, they continued, that things do not chop off suddenly at a dead end. What you are doing now carries over. No matter how temporary or expedient. It is to be finished: and it is to be useful for whatever else is to be done. Do not get the notion that be-

86

cause the job of the moment is evanescent, it is not worth bothering about; that you can skimp it; that any pains you bestow on it are wasted effort. It carries over.

Suppose, for instance, we have devoted an enormous concentration of study and effort in learning to sail a boat. Then we have to move inland, a thousand miles from water, for the rest of our lives. What we have to drive now is an airplane; and hardly one thing we have learned about handling boats fits in with handling airplanes. All that time wasted!

Nevertheless we are very stupid indeed if we do not realize that the time was not wasted. To be sure the skills of sheet and halliard, reef and spinnaker, tack and reach are useless. But the qualities we have developed in acquiring those skills come in very handy. Alertness; coolness; judgment; prompt muscular reaction; resourcefulness; courage; caution—we learned them on the water, we can use them in the air. Into our new habitation we have brought a pretty handy outfit after all. And we collected it on our boat, even if we had to leave the boat behind.

One thing we must realize, then, is that exactly this thing is true of all that we do in life: we are collecting an outfit which will be useful in a new habitation. There is the specific skill, which applies to the thing we are doing now; and also the intangible quality developed by the gaining of that skill. The intangible quality is part of the outfit for the new and strange country we are to inhabit.

"You remember the experimental dying," said the Invisible, "and how you set up housekeeping with the few things you had brought along of realities—volition, patience, perseverance, loving-kindness, whatever you had of enduring qualities—and by the exercise of them created new environment. Well, you don't have to go so far imaginatively as that. You can imagine yourself,

87

as happens to many, suddenly transplanted, an emigrant, a refugee, any example of a suddenly uprooted being hustled into a radically changed environment. Place yourself in imagination in Smyrna or Palestine or Timbukto or any other part of the world—without luggage! The success of your adjustment will be entirely dependent on the mental and spiritual capital you have brought with you.

"Consider one who is without firmly established supporting convictions, previously developed through his having constructed his own firm conditions of maintenance elsewhere; without the eternal verity of equilibrium; without the surrounding stability of confidence in his own power of re-establishing through summoning or magnetically attracting to himself the same replacement conditions anywhere. He will begin at once to disintegrate and throw into confusion his whole creative mechanism, by tearing it up into little worry-bits as to food and every detail as to present and future need, and his lack of possession of them at the moment. His panic over his mechanism of reconstructing his life puts him at once into the conditions he fears.

"Now what I am trying to get at is that your real wealth and capital, which will rehabilitate you in *any* change that comes to you, is the extent to which you have developed this inner reality. It is what gives strength to character, the power to convince and influence others, the calm acceptance of temporary destructions of one's impermanent possessions and surroundings."

"I get your point about character building," said I, "but that is long-range stuff—the job of a lifetime. Isn't there something more specific and immediate we can do to prepare ourselves?"

"The best safeguard I can give you," replied the Invisible, "is to put more time into thinking constructively of your new body. If you can realize clearly this core of life that carries on beyond your present span, and fulfill all your daily occupations and expenditures of strength in relation to it, that will help tremendously."

"Think of life as a shaft," Betty continued, "extending up into the sky out of sight, and ourselves as clinging around the very bottom of it. Our usual way is to mark it off in sections, like a barber's pole. But that is a very limiting idea. The biggest thing we can do for ourselves is to make a new conception of life as one continuous thing extending far beyond our present span. If you do that, you cannot mark off a line at the bottom of that shaft and say: these things I do are only for this span. Because whatever you do that you cannot feel sending you progressively forward, however slowly— that thing will become a bother to you.

"I wish everybody in this world would get together and raise this shaft to represent Life, and would look up to it every day and value the day's doings in relation to it. Then the oppression of this level of consciousness would be gone, and its lower standards and dwarfing ideals; and each moment would have a balance of all eternity."

Another aspect of this was presented to Betty in a symbolic experience so striking that I am going to conclude by quoting it here complete.

"Today I'm playing such a curious beautiful game," she said. "I'm putting together precious bits of memory-perfections....Such a curious jumble of things—memories of wide awesome spaces, and mountain tops, and flowing deserts, and young spring, and fragrances, and rosy babies—all the releasing memories I have on hand....

"I am learning how I shall use my earth experiences over here, the creative power of them when put together properly. They are building materials, just as brick and mortar are there. I pile up my memories and step on them, as it were, into a higher condition of perception. My precious sensibilities! I haven't half enough of them! I hunt around among my deepest and tenderest feelings, my intensest longings, all the parts of me that are most quivered with life. I wish there were a lot more; they make such a little bit of building material.

"My great longings take precedence; they are the readiest for fulfillment. All my satisfied memories support them and give them substance and structure. It is so vast. I make my selections of conscious participation by my great longings developed on earth, and by satisfying them develop others, thus gaining cognizance of still vaster possibilities....I feel like a yeast cake, or the building of a honeycomb, or something just made of the thought cells of experience. It would be terrible to come over without any intensities to build on.

"All this is to show us the way we are constantly preparing or neglecting our future building materials. The only way it can be demonstrated is through symbols of intensity, which is eternal life substance. You can continue to quicken yourself wholesomely, naturally, normally in every faculty—physical, mental, spiritual—each year freeing yourself, moving toward youth instead of age, the youth of your next and higher phase of life. It doesn't come through thinking; it isn't thinking, it's *doing*—like physical exercises, only these are everything: will, sensory, every kind of pleasurable participation in living vitally.

"I feel the difference just as you can tell electric current or when it's shut off; just as definite as that. This current is the intensity that runs through to our pleasures and beliefs and longings: the permeation of the spirit, which is so difficult to put into convincing words...."

She paused a few moments as though contemplating something, and then continued ruminatively.

"That's cowboy talk: to be afoot in a new country. I'd hate to be afoot in that new country. Parsimonious living here would put me afoot....That would be very awkward.

"Do you see what they're doing? They're showing us we must start here the machinery we're going to use there, so we won't be dazed and helpless immigrants. Poor immigrants: they're all right in their own country, but they have to go down the scale here because they aren't prepared. I certainly am grateful: at least I've got a familiar machine to make me go ahead wherever I am. I'm delighted, too, I can slide over so easily. Now I can die with savoir-faire."

"That," commented the Invisible, "is what all education and cultivation is, isn't it?—making you natural and at home, master of yourself in every situation."

"I wish," Betty concluded, "I could find words to tell you how pleasant and deep-breathed and natural and wide-experienced it is to live in constant relationship to the future. How can one speak about 'life beyond,' when *there is here?*"

PART TWO

DEVELOPMENT

The single thing I can get hold of today is the drabness of our life. Why don't we intensify it? There are not enough breathing spaces, like parks in a city; not enough moments of susceptibility to happiness and well-being. It's not punctuated; it's all run together with the details of life. If we could only make ourselves distribute more and more frequently through our hours little breathing spaces for the spirit to mount to consciousness of strength and well-being, that would be the training we need in the gradual acquisition of the happiness we won't take. But we shut it all out except for the occasional hour, and gradually the barrier thickens. We must keep it thin and easily broken through. It's the frequency, not the length of time, that does it.

The spirit and truth of reality I have received intuitively and am in more or less dumb possession of. But that doesn't amount to much except as a beginning. It is a nebulous sort of thing until backed up, and won't do any good unless I slowly grow the strength to sustain. Otherwise it will just run in and out, like the tide.

You see it is never wise to go any farther than you can get the strength to sustain, to maintain, to establish. Even the highest awareness that is purely spiritual amounts to little until you back it up.

CHAPTER I

DISTANT RANGES

After growing to the moment of ripeness, we must each discover our own way-in to the new country. But once we have done so, we may reach for, and find, the guiding beacons of predecessors. They are beacons, not cold monuments, and trace no path, but comfort by their assurance that we have the right direction.

Nevertheless I do believe that each will trace, *in some form*, the experience I have described. He will, *in some form*, receive a sudden illumination. This will vary in kind, from that of the fellow who merely ''sees it clearly at last,'' and kicks himself for having been so stupid; to the higher ecstasy said to irradiate seers and saints.

This insight, or ''revelation'' is, in its full clarity, rarely more than a flash, or a glimpse. For one fleeting instant we seem to *feel* that we know what it is all about. The moment passes; but the accompanying exaltation lingers. We begin to think it is permanent. We mistake the mood for a permanent state of being. From now on we are going through life a-tiptoe and a-tingle in vibrant exuberance. The load is lifted, the struggle banished. And the more confident of that we are, the more disconcerting, even dangerous, is going to be the reaction. For inevitably and inexorably we shall come down from tiptoe; our ecstasy is going to drain back to its earned level.

There is the danger point. Unless we understand that this exaltation of being is not a sudden free gift we are to keep, but an anticipation, a promise of what might be, and *will* be in due course and if we earn it; our failure to stay up there with the shining moment is likely to throw us into a violent revulsion against the whole subject. We accuse ourselves of illusion. We have been psychopathic: or weak; or unworthy. Such an attitude is foolish. It is dangerous, for it may drop us back to despair. And useless. We have not failed: how could we fail when we have not yet begun? We have stood at a lookout point in the foothills, and the day was clear, and we have seen distant peaks against the sky.

In the Navy they have a phrase that has always tickled my sense of quaintness. I first heard it thirty years ago. By courtesy of the Department I was on my way down the Lower California coast to attend the annual target practice at Magdalena Bay. It was evening. The Captain of the ship and I were gossiping in his cabin. Suddenly the lights all went out. We sat for a minute or so in darkness. Presently came the sound of the door opening, and then the voice of the orderly.

"Sir," said the latter, "the lights are out."

"Make it so," rejoined the officer.

After a brief interval evidently the trouble was found and remedied. Again the orderly appeared and saluted.

"Sir," said he gravely, "the lights are on again."

"Make it so," repeated the Captain.

The lights had been out, we had sat for some minutes

in the darkness: the repairs had been made, we had sat for half a minute in the light. But neither interim, or of light or of dark, had had any official reality. It had remained a mere potentiality until, from headquarters, the directing power, it had been "made so."

That is a fine and useful phrase: a fine and useful regulation to which we would do well to subscribe. It symbolizes grandly a basic truth. Make-it-so. Literally, no matter how substantial or how convincing the appearance, it has no reality unless we have made-it-so.

But in personal progress there is this difference from the Navy use of the phrase: we cannot make-it-so by mere approval.

It seems fairly obvious that Betty's early experiences of the higher consciousness were a kind of Cook's tour of as much of the region as she could take in. Conditions were carefully controlled so that her exploratory effort would not meet with too much resistance.

It is also fairly obvious, I think, that there could be little make-it-so in such first trips. One does not get title merely by walking through. The Invisibles pointed this out clearly. Occupation of the higher consciousness, said they, requires skill. The only way a skill can be developed is by *doing*, over and over—repetition, preferably with as little help as possible.

Accordingly Betty was assigned daily practice periods, during which she did her best to retrace her brilliant exploratory flights, but unaided, under her own power. In time she gained what appeared to be considerable proficiency. Still the Invisibles did not seem satisfied. Then one day the reason was disclosed. Here is the record:

Betty: (After a pause.) I can't understand this new crowd at all. There are such curious waits and consul-

97

tations and things. They seem to be preparing something different for me to do. I never can stay where I can successfully accomplish. I always have to go on beyond, and that makes it so much harder each time....

I've got to have so much surety and composure before they will begin. They won't waste any time or effort on anything that hasn't been prepared. I can't help myself. I just have to hang around....

Now at last I have reached the condition of confident happiness and strength I should like to be in always.

Invisible: That is all very well now, but suppose we put a strain on this acquired poise of yours. Would you stand the test, or would you go to pieces?

(Pause.)

Betty: They took me and put me in a terrible crowd. Ugh! Such a mass of humanity! I tried to push them all back to get a little of my own atmosphere around me. I struggled so hard!

Invisible: That is the life people have to struggle against.

Betty: I don't understand why I should be put through this. I can't get rid of it. I'm always brought back to humanity crowded like a railway station. So different from our calm, ordered life.

Invisible: Sensitiveness capable of absorbing wisdom through direct impression suffers enormously from the world of combat. For as awareness increases, so does suffering. A wider vision reveals not only rightness, but also the terrible wrongness. Because of this, unfortunately, the spiritual aspirant often prefers to seek a sheltered life and become a bystander. Unwilling to make what seem to him futile efforts at righting things, he prefers the refuge of passivity. Such a person may have an exquisitely sensitized vision, but he is absolutely sterile because of lack of human contact. One reason why the strength of unenlightenment is rampant is this shrinking of sensitiveness from contact with it. The bystander probably considers it fastidiousness, but it is really inertia, atrophied force, overcultivation, loss of productiveness.

Betty: I want to look at him again. He's quite fascinating, quite exquisite, but useless. If set in action, so much of him would break or crumble or change. What a pity he couldn't be used! He's such a highly developed specimen.

Invisible: He's got to learn to take his sensitiveness out of the way or he can't be put to work.

The whole point is, any sensitive person is useless in employing the force of the higher consciousness if he is always vulnerable to the return blows of the world. Suppose he is trying to accomplish something, and everybody begins irrelevant personal attacks, obstructions of all kinds. The minute he becomes susceptible to that he is automatically shut off from the power current which was going to *help* him accomplish.

You yourself must look out for this. You have gained access to a shining substance. Now you must learn to use it against a lower element superior in quantity. The toughening process which will make your bit of strength available must rest with you. Little by little, in small matters at first, you must learn to protect your mind against the darts and arrows which poison resolution.

(Pause.)

Betty: I feel as though I had grown exceedingly strong roots, recognized as an achievement in the root world, but with only a tiny visible shoot. Now I've got to make the visible growth balance the roots before I can go on to enduring attainment. The side of me that is visible must be made to exhibit the strength of my inner development....

Such a body blow to realize that what I have been able

99

to get is no good to anybody! My faith is stronger than ever, but it must stand a terrible ordeal and test—like snowflakes falling on a wet pavement.

Invisible: If you can carry on through this, all will be well. If not, you will sink with the rest. The great difficulty of all spiritual communion is the intermittence of it. Our end is dependent on the establishing of magnetic control from yours. That lacking, misunderstood, or thrust aside by circumstances of life, the conviction or quickening contact is gradually dimmed, sometimes to the point of extinction.

No suggestions are offered today. The problem is merely stated for your solution. You stand at the crossroads. Either you proceed faintly shadowed by a strange experience, or you strive onward toward a hold on the vitality of spiritual life which will remain unbroken even in the darkest hours of proof. That, you must realize, is your ultimate goal: *unbroken spiritual consciousness.*

The tiniest little bit of an effort really to accomplish, the crudest kind of a structure, is worth so much more than years of atrophied intellectual attainment. The crude little structure is a live thing. It can be extended and beautified indefinitely.

All that thought-power they talk about so scientifically is just each one's ability to move the different motes of his ego out into the sun. By his power of selecting his own motes of thought, of deciding which will be visible to him, he determines which will become the controlling motive of his actions. It is a great simple power, if you think of it that way—moving your motes in and out of the sun, throwing thoughts into shadow or into brilliant being, just as you please. It would make godlike beings of us.

CHAPTER II

TENDERFOOT

I soon realized Betty was not alone in her make-it-so problem: it was up to me, too. The only difference was that, whereas she had definite attainments to translate into everyday life, I had still to go through elementary school. Through Betty's records and other study, I had early gained at least a fair mental understanding of my aim. Just recently I had been given an actual small sensation of what I was after. But submitting to an apparently spontaneous and involuntary experience and commanding the technique to reproduce that experience at will are two different matters. Any dub can hit an occasional long drive, but it takes an expert golfer to turn in a qualifying score.

In other words—and obviously—there is not only the aim, but the method. Knowing where you want to go is all very well, but you must also know the right way to get there. The futility of mere good intention has been made into a proverb. I had seen—we all had seen—so many people sincerely, honestly, passionately, reaching toward expansion; ardently and arduously seeking the higher consciousness. They were wholly well-meaning. Their relationship to others, as far as they could make them so, were altruistic and selfless. Apparently here was no lack of intention nor wavering of aim. Yet somehow they had managed to miss out completely. Strange things happened to them, which they seemed not to deserve. Either they had turned queer and visionary; or joyless in a wrack of spiritual anxieties; or zealous with a certainty of self-righteousness. They either became helpless victims of spiritual wretchedness, or self-righteous proselytes of spiritual arrogance. They were both lonely and unhappy. And the search, to which they were still inexorably bound, had turned frantic and tormented. Doubly so since it seemed to them they had—as was indeed the case—lived singly in the purest intention.

This state of affairs, at first, rather disconcerted my sense of justice. Such steadfastness of purpose did not seem to deserve such penalty. But now I began to see some reason in at least some of their troubles. In the words of the Old-Timer, they were headed in the right direction, all right, but they were going the other way! Ignorance does not excuse. The desire of these people to get to the right place was sincere enough, but they had picked a dangerous trail.

Through the ages literally dozens of blueprints have been laid on our intellectual tables, each outlining in its own way some system of self-development. Properly used, each is effective. They vary greatly in risk. One such route is loosely designated as the "occult." History is peppered with accounts of initiations and mysteries and Yogi exercises and "concentrations" and

102

esoteric "disciplines"—all intended to help the aspirant on his way. Most of these are pretty drastic. Possibly that quality was demanded for the days when they were evolved. And by that very fact they are dangerous to the uninformed. So are powerful drugs in the hands of any but an expert physician. Like the drugs, they have their use. But one thing is sure: they should never be attempted, even by those to whom they are appropriate, without expert guidance. To do so is to invite unbalance and possible destruction.

Another approach is through the so-called "psychic," which presupposes the guidance of ex-carnate intelligence.

I use "so-called" advisedly. As we have already seen, "psychic" is a blanket term, and can cover about everything debatable, from table tipping and automatic writing, to trance mediumships. In its purest use it might be defined as Invisible guidance. Its worst has been so publicized that it has had a bad name with the orthodox. Nevertheless it is an effective route for those who are suitably constituted. Betty's approach is "psychic," for example. But like the "occult" route, it may be dangerous. To place oneself indiscriminately at the disposal of unknown forces and personalities is as silly as turning over all your money to someone you know nothing whatever about, and whom you have never even seen. There is always the possibility that you will come under wise and considerate care. But the chances are you will wake up one day to find you have attracted a crowd of thugs and incompetents, with no desires beyond using you for their own purposes. And that is not all, for even though awakened, you may by then find it next to impossible to free yourself of them. And that is a quick way to the psychopathic ward.

Nevertheless, I repeat, some individuals are so con-

103

stituted that "psychics" offers the most effective way to begin the journey, possibly the only way—for them. Of that we have little definite knowledge. But that it is risky we are *very* sure. One who picks this trail must make up his mind to watch his step and take it easy. Otherwise he is due for a bad smash.

A third approach is through exoteric religion. Any religion worthy of the name affords to those especially constituted a means of reaching the higher consciousness. Since they deal more in general principle and less in the details of instruction and process, as routes they are much less dangerous for use by the average man. But for that reason they are correspondingly less effective—and by no means altogether safe, at that. Plenty of people have gone "queer" over religion, and some have even become violent and had to be locked up. But so can one go crazy over almost anything. I had an aunt who went crazy over cats!

This vast field of tradition and knowledge, then—together with that outlined in the many hundred pages of instructions from the Invisibles to Betty—was what I found before me when I faced the question of method. It was enough to make any reasonable person pause and consider.

I think it was Ajax who begged merely that he might see the face of his enemy. And Davy Crockett who wanted to be right before he went ahead. I have always had great sympathy with both. That is why I myself circled this subject so warily, like an old mallard coming into a pond, before settling down into it.

Throughout Betty's training, as I have explained, I followed the instructions with the greatest care—intellectually. They made perfectly good sense, and I had little trouble understanding them. Nor were they at all complex or obscure. In fact, quite the contrary, they were so clear and simple as to be a little hard to hold onto. I found myself having trouble taking them seriously.

Later on I investigated quite a number of the "occult" systems in search of cross-lights. In this I was partially successful. Small bits here and there fitted in. Occasional heretofore unsuspected vistas opened out. As a whole, however, I was disappointed. All these systems seemed to me to boil down merely to obscure and mysterious and complicated ways of doing much the same things as had been explained more simply to Betty. Eventually the Invisibles summed it up for me neatly.

"The basic principles underlying all spiritual formulas," said they, "have been glimpsed in these teachings. All begin with the blank sheet, the wiping out of scattered impressions, such as bodily tensions and mind chasings—the creation of a little fair open space in which to put something better and more beautiful than our ordinary creations. All begin with this, whatever it is called. The next step is the vitality to preserve that space permanently, and gradually enlarge it. What comes to occupy the space thus fittingly prepared is the continual secret wonder of each individual life."

Compared with Betty's more advanced excursions, my own simple beginnings must seem elementary. Nevertheless I think they are worth quoting, as illustrative of one approach to the higher consciousness which is relatively safe. That doesn't mean it is foolproof: there is no such thing. But it should prove reasonably negotiable, I believe, to the average individual with ordinary stability and common sense.

Concerning the first step toward "getting out of the

body," I had found practically all instructions unanimous; one must begin with physical relaxation. Many of the systems I had investigated gave minute directions. One was to go over the body muscle by muscle, consciously smoothing the tensions from each. In time and with sufficient practice one was supposed in this way to gain the desired complete release.

I do not doubt that this is so. I even found such a procedure to be of considerable help to myself—in the very beginning. With sufficient will power I could, in time, make all my muscles behave. But was that relaxation? It did not seem to me so, logically. As I saw it, the idea was to withdraw attention from the body, not stand around vigilantly seeing that it carried on. And it was too much like dumbbells. I have always hated dumbbells.

Then it occurred to me to run things from a headquarters standpoint. The muscles are not my job: they are the body's job. Why not dispose of the body so that it could have no just cause for complaint; convey to it that I wanted to busy myself elsewhere and did not wish to be bothered and that it would be useless to complain; then just go there, leaving it to obey or not as it pleased.

I was not foolish enough to believe this system would work perfectly at once. I realized I would at first have to come back often to chide, help out, repeat instruction—to practice. But meanwhile I would at least be facing my underlying purpose whole: I would be trying to escape from my body.

Unfortunately this did not by any means solve the whole problem. Another requirement insisted on by all systems of spiritual development is the sweeping clean of the mind. The picture conveyed to me was of the driving out of a buzzing trivial swarm, and the throwing out neck and crop of any subsequent intruders. Most systems suggest an intense concentration on various objects for this purpose—"blanking out" on oranges or candle flames or crystals or what have you. The implication of all these methods seems to be an "excluding of the world" by some sort of drastic focusing of the mind.

Probably that works for some: I found it would not work for me. This job of throwing out irrelevancies meant vigilance. And vigilance and concentration, however effective they might be for the immediate purpose, defeated the ultimate purpose—for, to me at least, their exercise meant contraction. Possibly long, dull and painful practice would have enabled me to do these two opposed things at once. Like learning to pat the head and rub the stomach at the same time. But somehow the prospect tired me all out. It had, again, too much the flavor of dumbbells before breakfast.

Then came my second remarkable burst of illumination. If dumbbells for the body were no good, why dumbbells for the mind? Possibly chasing out each small trivial thought was the same as following around each trivial muscular tension. Why not use on the mind the same brilliant idea that had worked with the body? Why not just *abandon* the mind, its haphazard little thoughts, and all? Leave them down there, along with my body?

In this manner, I evolved and grew into a little daily routine. I would begin by lying flat on my back—preferably on the floor, because of its more stable support. Then for a brief space I would picture to myself various relaxing things: a dog flopped asleep in the sunshine, a cat stretched out before the fire, a coat on a coat-hanger, the sensations of floating in warm water or of falling comfortably through space. I practiced until I could do this promptly. I found that sometimes I could cut down the detailed technique to a momentary gesture in the general direction of what I wanted. On occasion, if I happened to be very tense, I might have to go back to first principles for a brief review. But the general tendency was for this step to become more and more subordinate and unconscious, like digestion. I could just go on about my business and trust it to take place automatically.

Then the mental escape; but this was not so easy. For one thing, a good strong thought-stream cannot be abandoned all at once. It has momentum. One cannot hop off it in full motion any more than one can hop off a railway train in full motion. It must be at least slowed down. Or, to change the figure, it is better to divert an unruly child than to clash with him.

Substitution is the answer. For example, I would repeatedly divert my attention to little discontinuous noises—a bird singing, the creaking of the woodwork, the wind passing in the trees. It had occurred to me that when one looks or listens or feels with his whole mind he does not think. Of course the thought stream kept reasserting itself, but each time its direction would be changed and its interest-momentum diminished.

Sometimes I would use memory pictures as the substitute: a tiny brook murmuring contentedly among the giant sugar pines; a green meadow in the enchanted silence of the forest depths; thin, rose clouds streaking a sunset sky; the shimmer of moonlight upon the summer sea. These, and their kind, I would pursue, until the thrill and the wonder of beauty had closed gentle fingers about my consciousness.

The next step had been hinted to me by the Invisibles: through Joan, of *Our Unseen Guest*. I must now, said they, carefully, very carefully picture myself as

108

floating unanchored in space. Various physical symbols helped. A bird high above the ground. An airplane in space, touching nothing. A balloon in the stratosphere. One picture that seemed to be particularly effective was that of smoke rising slowly and hanging under the ceiling. As long as my interest was centered in these, no bustling thoughts came to disturb me.

Last of all I would carefully, very carefully, detach myself from my symbols and try to sense myself as a disembodied point of consciousness in space. Surprisingly, this wasn't too hard to do, though at first the effect stayed with me only for an instant. The moment strain set in I abandoned the attempt, descending easily of my own specific gravity, like a glider settling back to earth. Then rest for a moment comfortably in my habitual self, contemplation of a few pleasant unrelated thoughts, and another try.

"This training," said they, "is really bringing the subconscious, which has charge of your automatic actions, under some sort of responsible discipline. When this is accomplished, it will no longer be necessary to spend your time with it in the nursery.

"The subconscious is an executive thing only; it carries out. It is enormously efficient, but it acts only on stimulus and guidance. Lacking your intelligent stimulus and guidance, it takes what offers. Untrained, its tendency is to usurp. Unresisted, it carries the conscious mind down its own channel of interest. You notice this when you are trying to concentrate on some line of thought, and are constantly distracted and carried off down extraneous lines. The remedy is not will-power forcing, but a good-humored detaching, as from the importunate hands of children. The ease and good-humor of the detachment depend on whether or not the children you are dealing with are trained or spoiled.

"In the routine you have been following you are also training your conscious mind, not in specific detail, but in the direction of habitual association with the super-conscious rather than the subconscious. Standing between the two, it has its choice."

The secret of success with the reinforcing power of the higher consciousness is to practice with it as a recreation. Then when the time comes you can test its reality by deliberately selecting an upsetting moment, a harassed moment, and applying it purposefully. But before you can use it in serious matters, you must first use it for your own pleasure. Otherwise, it won't hold up.

CHAPTER III

PERMANENT CAMP

California today is a proudly organized civilization. Her productions fill long tables of statistics. She offers to her people a variety of habitation and of recreation to suit any possible taste; from Death Valley to the Redwoods of Humboldt; from surf riding to skiing. Her wildernesses are still vast, but trailed and rangered and administered and kept satisfactorily untamed.

Yet in my own recollection and experience California was still a frontier. There were no paved highways. The main roads were sketchy wagon tracks. Secondary highways did not exist. In their stead were trails on which we rode horseback. The Sierra, now speckled with resorts, searched through by wide ranger-made trails, criss-crossed with arterials, were to be explored only by pack train over the rough ways-through "monumented" for their own convenience by the sheep-and-cattle-men. And you did it yourself. Such a thing as a professional guide did not exist. And when you started, you stocked up for the duration, even to such things as horseshoes. There were no wayside stores.

Ordinarily the traveler camped where the night found him, improvised what he could not carry, changed his home every day, and to a great extent, "lived on the country." Once in a while he found it convenient to establish a base, a headquarters, from which to start out and to which to return. One could store things there. One could build something more substantial than a bivouac in case the elements got too rough. We did this. We even put up a cabin, with a fireplace, and a split rail fence, and other fancy fixings. It was a substantial, comfortable habitation; but it did not tie us. We still wandered far afield, among the great peaks. However, it was there; something permanent, something of our very own to which to return.

That is the general course of pioneering anywhere. Frontiers vary, but the process of their development does not. The case is no different, even when the frontiers are those of consciousness. Certainly Betty's exploration of them and occupying of them followed these classic lines.

Betty: Today I am in a very high order of consciousness and creative force, and I don't know what you are going to think about it. There is always such a gap. It is a very advanced idea they are preparing.

Invisible: The sensation of the inner psychic being is what we are after. In struggling to make words contain extensions of knowledge, we have to build very carefully in order not to lead astray.

Within every individual is a psychic core to which he can return in case of trouble. It is his enduring center, his seed that will endure. Search yourself for this constant within. You cannot play on your outer surfaces and pretend that they are it, because they are not. Nor will you find it in your brain. Look for it rather in the region of the heart; or more accurately, the intangible sensations which have no organic position. Warmth is the nearest we can come to describing it—a sort of cen-

112

tral heating idea. A continuous radiation always comes from the furnace, but when it gets out to the surface it cools off.

Betty: What they want now is to make me work on this until I realize it for myself.

Invisible: The practice of it is a withdrawing of one's efforts from the periphery of one's life to the center, and starting out again from there. You abandon for the moment all your hobbies and pursuits and interests and pastimes, leaving them scattered around as a child leaves his playthings, and enter your own self.

Betty: The way it feels to me is that all the things on the outside are thrown into a kind of blurred consciousness. It is pulled over them like a covering, and I've withdrawn into a region of intense radiation and well-being and power.

Invisible: This is the great security, the foundation for any superstructure of effort you may want to build.

You see, the great question is: How are you going to stabilize yourself among all the shifting pursuits of the world, the varied points of view, the conflicts and uncertainties? How are you going in the midst of them to reach the absolute reality? And the only answer is first to make within yourself an individual bit of reality over which you have complete jurisdiction. That is your one method of approach to the ultimate attainment of absolute reality.

The first step in control, then, is the possession of such an inner fortress for protection and refreshment. The nature of it can be described in many ways, but the main thing to acquaint yourself with is a feeling of liberation and immersion in complete security and power and warmth and beauty of happiness. Continually practice on this ideal nucleus, enlarging it, enriching it, intensifying its atmosphere with your accumulated memories of harmonious moments of life.

113

There is nothing more important than creating this abode of emotional security, spiritual order and demonstrable stength. Pain and struggle, the battle of life, are but half. The other half of life you work on slowly by means of illuminated bits of days, mere bits of hours in days, put together until the result becomes the inner strength. It is the establishing of this safe sanctuary—this sort of room of heaven within you—it's the accustoming of yourself to living part-time in it, that makes you able to go forth armed with a wisdom and power which is beyond your conscious mind to comprehend.

(Pause.)

Betty: Funny! I can't describe that. But it's a good deal like slowing up when you see a big policeman. The feeling of a person who is backed by this power slows you up the same way, if you are trying to overrule or influence him.

There is a certain respect for law, superior force, that regulates the lesser problems automatically. They don't capture you because they don't dare. They can't arouse that annoyance, that irritation, and make a captive of you, because you have your force behind you. Your big policeman has a competent look about him that carries conviction and turns the scale of capture. Instead of being overcome, you can act on the other fellow who tries to annoy you. But everybody picks on a person who has no protecting force. In the physical world it is the same....

This feeling of sureness and happiness and power that comes over me they want to call *authority*. It is not the word I'd use. They say they want to freshen the idea of authority.

Invisible: It is not the arrogance of a policeman backed by the law, nor the strength of an army. It is the wisdom of a just judge administering the laws of cause and effect.

114

(Pause.)

Stewart: See if I get the general idea. The human consciousness exists in two spheres and functions in both. The center of consciousness is usually in the earth sphere, and functions in the other indirectly, as one might say. But it is possible with advantage to establish a directing center in the other sphere. Is that it?

Invisible: Yes, yes. The object is to learn so to place your consciousness that it is strongly above earth frets. That is the ultimate desirable. It makes you one with the great creative forces of the universe, and brings a joy and strength such as you have never dreamed of. Before it the earth-fret becomes just a shadow of reality, just a shadow.

The world attacks everything from outside; and you are apt to meet that attack in detail from the outside too. This is an attempt to make you realize that your response must be from the inside out. You withdraw yourself. Things surge beneath, picking and battering and fuming, but they cannot destroy you. As long as you have this inner power you needn't mind who is battering on you, nor what tools or dynamite they are using. They can only be a surface nuisance. They may take the empty shell, but you have withdrawn the part of you they can hurt.

Of course this is difficult to do at first. Nevertheless that is the idea. Establish your inner desirable; and then when your undesirables appear you can turn your attention on your already established desirable. This "facing the enemy" is no good. *Ignore* the enemy and he is so reduced in stature that he cannot reach up and scratch you.

Betty: I am working on just two things: how to liberate myself at will, and how to retire to my inner

115

fortress. I can't do either, really. I can just experiment, and occasionally, as I succeed, I can notice how it happened.

Invisible: If you would gain true self-possession, take your moments of discord and entanglement, when all the irritations of the lower order of things exercise a kind of capillary attraction which seems to fasten you hopelessly to them—take these moments as your moments of practice in spiritual control. At such a time, how are you going to possess yourself; to reorganize and harmonize this entangling condition; to act, by your ability to free yourself from it, masterfully *upon* it instead of slavishly *in* it?

There is only one way, but you must have prepared it beforehand and practiced it: let go your hold of everything and withdraw yourself into the magic-working center of life within yourself. It is always possible to check your nervous reactions momentarily by suddenly commanding a relaxation, like making yourself stop shivering. Then quickly combine this momentary release with a swift retreat to your inner citadel. Go apart in it and rest the tensions. Stay in peace and quiet of volition, acquiescing in your whole being to the reharmonizing power of your higher consciousness. It is to the ordinary faculties as an adult sympathetic mind to a child's trouble. It helps you clarify your vision and gather strength to make your decisions and plan your actions.

This process you should regard as an emergency exit which you must have already in working order. In the confusion and involvement of actual combat it is almost impossible to improvise. Therefore to be effective you must, through your creative powers, already have so frequently experienced the most intense sensation of harmony and well-being within your fortress, that you can voluntarily re-enter the sensation even in moments of violent irritation. Your habit-serving consciousness must be so trained that association of ideas instantly reproduces the modifications in your brain which will allow you to escape at will from even the most discordant situations.

Betty: It is terribly important to practice running to your inner fortress at all sorts of odd times, the way you practice your golf swing. After a while it gets grooved that way. Then when a real problem comes along, when the ball is in front of you, you instinctively and naturally do the right thing.

Of course it takes lots of practice to fly quickly from your world life, when it gets obstructed, to your inner fortress. But it can be done readily after a while. You can drop your world life and climb to your fortress and look down on world affairs, and then you've got your perspective again. The more you do it the easier it gets.

Invisible: You must develop this self-security if you desire mastery. The complications and trials and demands of bodily existence can be overcome and directed only by the genius of your higher established life. And a correct estimate of temporary sensations of the body is to be obtained only through your ability to observe them and appraise them from your inner security. By recreating for yourself, even momentarily, the harmony of deep breath and refreshment within your inner fortress, you are empowered to return vitalized and armored against the discords. Without this inner fortress one is unborn into eternity, ungerminated in the higher life, unpossessed of oneself, acted upon but not motivating.

The subconscious cannot be coerced or browbeaten. It must be led pleasantly and gently. Therefore mere determination to do a thing, to reconstruct ourselves, is fatally prone to discouragement and failure. We have got to have a human and pleasurable system of pastimes which will help ourselves to succeed.

CHAPTER IV

BLAZED TRAIL

It is comparatively easy to be a Saturday's Hero; to be noble on especial occasion. It is quite another matter to be even moderately worthy when pegging back and forth on the familiar track of hourly trivialities. We may be following the path by means of the Shining Light, but routine seems to dim it; and the first thing we know we are off in the bushes.

The Invisibles must have anticipated something of the sort. They do not miss many tricks. For no sooner had they showed Betty how to reach her inner fortress, than they set about marking the trail plainly. And the markers they used were imaginative symbols.

This appealed to me. Thin air as a refuge in tough weather struck me as inadequate, at least for beginners. But definite symbols were more in my line. At least they offered something more or less concrete to reach for.

One of the first of these symbols dealt with a very elementary phase. The idea seemed to be that, if Betty was to escape easily to her sanctuary, resistance must be diminished. The grip of certain qualities which tended to hold her back must be weakened. Under-

118

brush must be penetrated, and a way cleared.

At its simplest this is no new idea. We have always recognized that we should control our tempers, rid ourselves of irritation, uncharitable thinking, egocentricity and all that brood. The accepted method has been to go forth and wrestle with the devil, in good old Biblical fashion.

As an effort this is praiseworthy enough, and undoubtedly we acquire merit by making it. But it is hard work, and discouraging, and too often we are thrown for a loss. The Invisibles had a better suggestion.

Invisible: You have certain traits which prevent your winning through to spiritual ease, and which you'll have all your present span of life. They are more than individual—they are racial. The more you attempt to thrash them, the more nerve strain there will be. But the less you combat them at all, the stronger they'll get. Therefore the only thing to do is to find a way around them by strategy. Granting that there is an expansive method which will in time overcome everything, still it is sometimes better to begin with more intimate methods.

One way is to regard the combat as something in the nature of a humorous private sport. You have no enmity toward the traits you are opposing, only a determination to prove your mettle. This technique gives a certain flexibility in turning from one consciousness to the other, and evades the tensions which come from unnatural spiritual straining.

(Pause.)

Betty: I didn't know how to go about it, so I made a friendly antagonist of my lower self, as one does in sports—in tennis, for instance—an antagonist one would be friendly with in other moments. For the time being he merely furnishes a conflict necessary to the developing of one's power. He becomes a kind of effigy.

119

Sometimes he is getting cross at the telephone, sometimes he is persuading me to hustle and not take time to breathe calmly and be relaxed of tensions, sometimes he is making me eat stupid things. It is far more amusing than being that self.

Invisible: All the usual methods of controlling oneself have a lack of grace and humor and amusement which desiccates their lifeblood. Therefore, to explain in commonplace fashion a method of approaching one's inner security, this harmonious and gracious stability, we offer the example of a game with one's friendly antagonist, one's 'lower self.' It is perhaps a misnomer to use the term 'friendly.' The friendliness is on the side of your higher self, for the lower is quite inferior in the type of his sportsmanship. He is quite inclined to malice toward his aristocracy!

Betty: The trick is in contemplating one's lower self as one stops to train and play with a puppy. I don't know why lower selves should always be considered vicious. Actually they have very engaging qualities. They are just uneducated.

Invisible: In this phase of development, as in all others, one must pass through the tinhorn-rattle-whistle stage of children playing games. One has to pass through it composedly, giving a due and proper comprehension of the necessity for games at all ages. In time you will find yourself able to lay aside your symbols and seek your goal direct, but do not rush prematurely into abstractions. The games and toys of children are among their best means of learning. Grownups do not play with toys; but taking away a child's toys does not make a grownup.

The Invisibles suggested various "games" for Betty to play—physical symbols to help her make her getaway. One day they recalled a familiar figure in a wider application.

Invisible: Human corrosives sometimes get so bad you can't assort and arrange and reharmonize them yourself. They have reduced you to their level in the most satanic fashion. You are all curdled with acidity mentally. Even though you recognize your plight and want to abandon it for a better attitude of mind, still you can't. What are you to do then?

At such times there are various ways of helping yourself to escape to your inner fortress. For example, you may not be able actually to go up in an airplane, but at least you can picture yourself there. In imagination you can look at the hills and valleys and shores and the little chicken-coop houses for a while. And then you can pityingly say: 'In one room of that little hive of a house there's an obstinate, irritated, inverted soul who thinks life is as he sees it, hard and bitter. But it is only his weakness and lack of the breathing in of life which has made him pervious to ferments.' Keep looking at that airplane picture. By degrees your attention will be so centered on the sweep of horizons that you will ignore, and thus liberate from his pitiable paucity, the man in the little room in the chicken-coop house.

You've got to keep an airplane tied up outside, like a horse, in case you need it. You can't stay up in it, perhaps, but when you come down you're full of oxygen and the winds in heaven, and are tolerant in proportion. You have escaped from your little self, and can treat it like a fretful child. You will have assurance and imperviousness to the ferments of others.

You see how much of it is in your own hands. If you want to shut the window and be relaxed into unoxygenated irritability of lesser life, you can. It is no sin: it is just your own loss. It is just ignorance of vision, the triumph of old habits, a deliberate delaying of your progress. You can always stay in your hall bedroom of the universe and contemplate its ill-furnished stuffiness, fixing your mind firmly on your cramped condition of life! That is your prerogative. But if you do, you belong to the spiritually illiterate.

Another interesting symbol was suggested for use in emergencies, when everything else failed:

Betty: Here I am in my citadel. I want to stay here and establish myself firmly and permanently. But suppose I get a panic or get weak. Then I cannot help myself. I've lost my balance. I am at the mercy of the lower elements. I am sinking....

What can I do now?...

Oh, I see! I'll pretend that, while I can't swim, I can put on an emergency life preserver. Something will hold me up under the arms until I can *think back* to what I've lost. It is an appeal to something outside myself to hold me up until I can get back again. I can depend on it. The life preserver symbol helps get the idea inside me. It is so important to get these ideas *inside* you.

There is also an idea that goes with it that I don't see very clearly. It has to do with paying for that life preserver sometime by putting forth great exertion, great effort to hold up somebody else. I don't understand that very well. But you can't get this help for nothing. With it you get some privilege of helping another. Privilege? I thought you were going to say penalty....

I've been struggling and am tired. It is difficult sometimes to sustain yourself here, but it's a pleasant exertion. It's like swimming, in that you know you are not in your accustomed element, and that your sustainment depends on your exertions....

That's a good idea, that one about maintaining yourself as in swimming. It helps to keep you from slumping back and drowning in all sorts of world things. Effortless peace is worthless. It should be stimulated harmony, not effortless peace.

Day after day, for many weeks, the Invisibles kept hammering away at this technique of escaping to the inner fortress. The imagery is too various to quote in full here, but another example or two might not come amiss. The following, for instance, casts an interesting sidelight on the main theme.

Invisible: There is a trick to hurry—we are talking of legitimate hurry. A good deal of hurry is unnecessary, and therefore silly. But even when hurry is indicated, the *method* of hurry is generally ridiculous. We will give you an example:

You are just short of the end of a block. For some reason it is very desirable that you get to the crossing before the light turns red. Your brain-mind so informs your body. Your body answers by more rapid movement, and the faithful subconscious gets busy raising the heart rate and the adrenal secretions and all the rest of your chemistry to meet the increased activities demanded by the occasion. Everything is being done by everybody to get you to that corner in time.

Well and good. What then? Instead of letting it go at that, your brain-mind then races ahead to the crossing, and dances first on one foot and then on the other, and shouts and urges and agonizes because *you* cannot be there before the whole of you is there; and the body leans forward and pours out energy and strains and frets because its physical speed cannot catch up with the speed of thought—which should be self-evident. And *you*—the eternal you that is your real self—where are you? Probably you are racing back and forth between

123

the two; or trying to divide yourself between the two, sharing the impatience of one and the impotence of the other; or spread out thin between them striving to drag them together by force of will. Psychically you are scattered out all over that block; and if that—from our point of view—isn't a ridiculous sight, I never saw one!

If you have any control over that brain-mind of yours, you will impress on it that its dignified role is first to point out the emergency, then to set in motion the machinery, after which to let the machinery get there, if it can. Stay together—all three of you—since none of you can get there, completely, without the others.

But even if you have a spoiled-child or only partly disciplined brain-mind, there is no earthly reason why you should go scuttling off with it. Deplore its fool actions, and let it go. Elect to stay with the body. Lean back luxuriously and comfortably and allow it to carry you until you catch up. Incidentally you will be a great comfort to your consciously laboring and somewhat bewildered subconscious. The poor thing is otherwise all distracted that it should still be urged and belabored when it is doing its best. After a few experiences you may, between the two of you, make that jittery brain-mind of yours ashamed of itself, so it will stay back where it belongs.

This admittedly frivolous example carries in itself a mightier general principle of living than at first appears. It is that of *rest in movement*. All living is, must be, movement of some sort. But the appropriate mechanisms of that movement, whatever it may be, carry with them on their shoulders a comfortable seat on which *you* may be borne in that timeless serenity which is the inner eternal essence of all there is.

One point in this escape business that caught my

124

curiosity was as to just how far it was effective. Did it apply to all occasions? Was it the best course to pursue in every case, or were there times when it wouldn't work? The Invisible's answer was unequivocal:

Invisible: In resisting the assault of discord, the most effective course is always to escape from the restrictions of your lower self, as you call it, by merging with the greater freedom of the inner consciousness. But the line of least resistance is always the slipping back into one's lower self, and becoming aware merely of momentary sensations. This drag is ever-present. Do not give in to it through laziness or forgetfulness. It is a constant temptation to sink back into the momentary sensation.

Stewart: Nevertheless the momentary sensation sometimes forces attention. How about pain, for instance, real and absorbing pain?

Invisible: Only in health, in equilibrium, in balance of powers can self-elevation be achieved. The rousing of physical discord produces a painful disorganization almost impossible to overcome without previous training. At such a time, the straining of attempted control by will-power merely defeats the purpose. That is a great and tragic mistake. Pain must be relaxed to and passed through a flooding-out process, washing it away, easing it by nonresistance. Resistance seals it from healing forces, inhibits the throwing off as well as the replenishment. A will-power fight against pain is a very tragic sight. *Never tighten up!*

Stewart: You say that only in health can self-elevation be achieved. By that do you mean that invalids are barred from it?

Invisible: No. Any effort toward the related consciousness permits a vitalizing by its superior force which tends to overcome momentary sensation. But the practice of it in times of equilibrium, establishing the habit, will greatly aid its automatic action when disorder comes.

Do not resist pain. Begin there. This does not mean to give up and let pain take whole possession. But to relax to it. Allow it to descend on a strong conviction of its transitory nature. This opens floodgates which dilute the force of pain and gradually dissolve its power. It will then be seen to spend itself merely on your surface consciousness, however all-absorbing that surface may previously have seemed during suffering. But it is in *times of health* you must develop the conviction of the transitory nature of pain which will uphold you when it floods over and seems to take possession of your life. Then when it comes you can afford to let it flood, just keeping open the gates which will soon clear the turgid stream.

Fundamentally, life and all its experiences pass through you like radio waves, and you are not affected by them. It is only your resistance to them that damages you. Therefore if you can just let them pass through you, and assert yourself of higher substance, you can take them in quantity, from the most exalted honors to the direst calamities. In themselves, they are as little disintegrating as shade on your body: they are just fleeting phenomena. Never object to any experiences if you can attain to that. The more they come, the more honored you are in your selection of apprenticeship.

I am going to conclude this chapter with a record which seems to me to give a peculiarly intimate glimpse of Betty's experience. Like a glimmer of distant lightning at night, it hints at something beyond the horizon of our present awareness.

Betty: (after a pause) There's getting to be such a big

126

gap between the way the ordinary human being thinks and the stratum of thought I am in now. I wonder if it's worth the struggle. It sounds so unreal and absurdly imaginative to you. I'm a little discouraged lately about saying it, because it doesn't take effect.

(Pause.)

I'm getting a terrible lesson on discouragement, a *terrible* lesson! Letting in the jungle! They say nobody's going to clarify it all unless I give vitality to it and bring it out of the fog. It is the strength to do this I am working on now. I am just discarding everything in a great rush of desire for this best and highest, which I sense as a great strength. There's so little recognition around me of this obtainable power. Nobody wants it enough to suffer for it, and I want it so tremendously it makes me seem set apart and strange and inhuman.

Nevertheless, this inner strength is the only means of recognizing one's lower self, and by definite intake of inspiration lifting out of it; like the simple definite process of getting out of a chair or climbing stairs. I am just getting so I dread that faded lesser image of myself. When I get down into it, everything pours in on my weakness to torment me. My concave attitude is a receptacle for the weaknesses of others....

Now I turn the other way, by means of my strength. I present a different surface to life—convex. I have appeasement now; I have ease. I have magnified that bit of strength which is mine. What a strange thing that it's the great reality to me, the thing I must pursue, regardless of anything else. Because, until more of it is mine, I cannot exhibit it or give it.

And then there is that world of curiously unsubstance things around me.

Stewart: Unsubstance things?

Betty: On earth. How could you tell anybody that all those unsubstance things we do and putter with and

127

play with are only the shadow of what we are actually creating in this great strength we do not see? They are experimental samples of life we look over and play with for selective purposes. Ordinarily they are the only reality we recognize, but from here they seem just shadows.

To me the only enduring reality is my bit of strength. It is such a tiny bit, but it's a citadel I can live in, and from which I can go out on both sides of consciousness. In time, perhaps, I'll establish it as a permanent home. Then when I die, I'll just shut that other door and move freely on the other side.

The recognition of the things you desire, the forming of your definite purposes, establishes a condition as automatically chemical in its action as establishing the arrangements of any other chemical process, such as the release of gasses or the carbonization of flame or the boiling of water. It immediately starts toward the fulfillment of the desire in proportion to the strength, fervor and persistence of your effort toward it.

CHAPTER V

PASTURE

The attainment of understanding is always an interesting process. To the beginner skill seems to be an extended series of separate steps, to each of which in turn he must devote painstaking performance. But the object of his performances, as an ultimate unit of which they form the parts, eludes him.

In time, however, he discovers that daily practice squeezes out this separateness, as it were, until at last the various steps of process shorten to the compass of a single stride.

So it was with me here. For quite a long time I followed faithfully my beginner's routine. Each day, carefully, I repeated the detailed processes of physical relaxation, mental extrication and imaginative release. Then one day I suddenly found I needed no longer to go through this threefold process. A single brief mental gesture sufficed to lift me to the state of detachment and equilibrium which had been my objective. This revelation came as a distinct shock of surprise. Also, curiously, it made me feel somewhat foolish. Here I had been practicing away for weeks and months, off and on, and it was actually as simple as opening my eyes!

Nevertheless, I realized that I had reached an important milestone on the way.

About here I discovered another interesting characteristic of the expansion of consciousness. Like most other activities of life, it proceeds in a rhythm. There is a pulsation to it, a systole and diastole. After each definite acquisition is pause for its establishment, its incorporation in ourselves, its use and enjoyment for itself. The stream of our progress enters a quiet pool for clarification in the still depths until, presently, it yields to the pull of the downstream current.

So now, for an interval, forward progress seemed to have stopped. I kept on about the business of creating my "little fair open space," but for a time nothing exciting came to occupy it. That was all right. I was satisfied. The sense of repose and equilibrium into which the routine had led me was a sufficient reward in itself. I had come to look forward to it eagerly. But for a while nothing new turned up.

Then one day the Invisibles apparently decided that I was due for a little more personal instruction. Through Joan they moved in again. It happened at the time that I was suffering from a resurgence of a tropical fever I had caught in Africa. For this reason, perhaps, the instruction centered around what seemed to be a method of healing; though, as will be seen, the healing aspect was merely a peg on which the whole philosophy could hang. For that reason I am going to quote in some detail. Together with the preceding chapter, the quotations illustrate well the Invisible's way of instructing. When they have wished to lead us into some new field of reality, they have marked the way with imaginative symbols. Only the first step, the release from the body, is in all cases the same. After that the higher consciousness seems to open into a variety of different regions. The region to which we attain is determined largely by our purpose of the moment and the type of symbol we select as a means of approach.

"You are now able," began the Invisibles on this occasion, "to move your consciousness temporarily out of your body. In the vitalizing exercises we are about to suggest, it will no longer be necessary to devote your entire attention to this process. After rising above your body you will leave in that phase only the shred of awareness necessary to keep your airplane engine going.

"Resting easily in this state, you will first direct your attention to the universal life force. Think of it as a river connected with the blood stream in your body: a constant vital current flowing all through you, not fast, but in rhythm of a river. You do not *think into existence* the process of the vital flow by any applied effort of the imaginative will. It is more as though you simply noted the fact. The process is facilitated by your attention, but is not inaugurated by it.

"The next step has to do with making your acceptance of this universal vital stream more effective. Its aliment is not best absorbed by your body as a mere hash or soup of everything. Your diet should be various and discriminating: it should be like your physical diet, selective. Next, therefore, you will picture to yourself some great abundance, such as groves of fruit, vineyards, the coming harvest. If, in sympathetic imagination, you can touch your kinship with any given form of abundance, you can partake of its power. And since, in this world of abundance of which you think imaginatively, the distillation of the universal vital force is various, you are enabled in this way to partake of the aliments suited to your particular needs."

I'll admit that my first reactions to this advice were a trifle confused. Also, to begin with, I was singularly unsuccessful in trying to carry it out. Somehow my attempts to get in touch with agricultural products did not progress beyond the sort of kinship once described as "first cousin instantly removed." After I had dutifully kept at it for a while, I began to realize that I was verging toward strain. As I had at least learned *that* lesson, I at once let up.

While I was resting, my mind wandered idly to an Alaskan river I had once explored, and where I had had extraordinary good luck in my camera hunting of the big Kodiak bear. It was a beautiful river, and I spent much time recalling one by one the details of its topography. I had such a good time at this that it was only with difficulty I at length impatiently shook myself free from what I thought was too long an indulgence in "daydreaming." Back to the job!

But right there was where I made my big mistake. As it turned out, just when I threw the thing overboard—just at that very moment—I was beginning to succeed!

"We showed you," said the Invisibles afterward, "in minute detail of shallow and ripple and crossing and pool, one of your Alaska rivers; and you were impatient with yourself because you thought your 'mind was wandering.' But that, for a moment, and as an example, was a specific distillation of a specific form of abundance. Your mistake was in *willing* your imagination toward some particular form of abundance because we had suggested it as an example. Actually this selection lies in the province of the greater wisdom of your own superconsciousness, and is no more an affair of your brain-mind than is the varied use of the constituents of your blood stream in the nourishment of your body.

"In proceeding with this exercise, therefore, your attention must be permitted to *saunter*. It will then be attracted toward the need of the moment. There is, of course, a distinction to be drawn between this and idle wandering; a distinction that can be understood only through the actual experience. Basically there must be a certain alertness of spiritual appetite. But the subject of your reverie is determined by your spiritual instinct, and not through your intellectual interests or appraisements."

The hour which I was at present devoting daily to my routine now took on a new fascination. As I have said, by this time I was able to "take off" promptly and easily, rising quickly above attention to both my body and my usual thought activities. Then, having suspended myself, as it were, I could free-heartedly turn to the delightful pastime of "letting my mind saunter," to see what today it would attract. I never knew what that was to be, but once it had established itself my fancy drifted into a peculiarly agreeable contemplation of it. It was much like stepping from shade into warm sunshine. If the expression does not sound too fantastic, it was a good deal like basking in an idea.

One day this basking took on an almost literal form. On the occasion in question my point of attention-attest was very simple. I was merely in a bath of that peculiarly soaking sun-warmth that floods California's interior valleys just before the great heats of summer.

"This," said they later, "is the most potent physical abundance of all. It is abundance in its purest form. It is the origin and source of all physical abundance as a moments's reflection will show you. But as such it must be thought of and used sparingly only as a refreshment of sheer vitality. It is too pure an essence for sole diet. For purposes of physical building it must be appropriately transformed into variation; just as it is transformed by mineral, plant and animal before it becomes physically nourishing as food for human specializations, each after the manner of its own construction. You cannot eat sunlight, yet sunlight is the source, the life force, of physical life. What you eat is sunlight transmuted through your fellow creations in the physical world.

"As a rule, then, abundances should be associated with the idea of ripeness. Only culmination, ordinarily, is fit to be appropriated. Ripening is the business of the individual; until it reaches the culmination point, it is not a subject for ingestion."

As, indeed, why not? We know enough not to eat green apples.

On another occasion my mind's sauntering brought me to recollection of a great waterfall. It was a smooth sheet of water at its brink, not very wide, but of considerable volume. A third of the way down it admitted the air to spread into a widening lace-work of spray and down-shooting hesitating arrows. A dark forest leaned across its channel to look. A dark pool received and quieted it again. The whole air pulsed with its deep and solemn roar, which, nevertheless, mysteriously did not disturb a certain cathedral hush.

I had known that waterfall well, I had stood in the spray of its mists at the pool below. I had scrambled and fought my way up through the tangle of its precipice to the upper waters. Today, in my recalling of it, I poised in imagination just off the brink of its plunge. It was a delightful picture; but as an example of "abundance," in the exact sense of my present technique, it seemed a little doubtful.

"This manifestation of abundance," explained the Invisibles afterward, "is that of a combination of many powers, instead of but one. The plunge of the waterfall is the combination of the force that has lifted the vapor from the sea, the various forces that have made the winds to move, the airs to cool, the clouds to condense, the rain to fall, the stream to flow downhill, until at the brink of the plunge is a great and mighty and resistless abundance of actual power that may be breathed-in as a single thing, an element of refreshment and vitality. This is a good example of what we meant by a *distillation* of abundance. It has by these many processes been prepared for spiritual ingestion, just as the varied elements comprised in physical foods are concentrated by natural processes in the grain of wheat."

In similar fashion on succeeding days my mind "sauntered" to stop at the ceaselessly intermittent hovering crash of breakers on a shore, wind in trees, and the like until, to my own amusement when I thought of it afterwards, I did come back satisfactorily to the agricultural business I had at first rejected. Ripe fields of grain; orchards heavy with fruit; the lavishness of spring gardens—after all is said and done, those *are* the nearest symbols, if one can use them—of abundant lavish life expressing itself, pouring itself out in the fecundity of mother earth.

That was all there was to these particular experiences. Over a period of weeks they recurred regularly. The imagery of my private movie varied, but it did not seem to progress toward any perceptible culmination of either intensity, significance or duration. Each day at the end of about the usual interval the strength of my suspension always waned. I yielded to what was still my specific gravity, and drifted gently back to my ordinary habitation. Sometimes I had an elusive momentary conviction that the index of my capacity had risen just a little—perhaps was destined to rise. But for the present this went no further. It remained just a vague premonition, in the penumbra of my consciousness. Following the exercises nothing persisted except a heightened sense of vitality and well-being. Gradually my health improved.

Then one day the Invisibles again signed off. But before doing so they added one final piece of advice.

"You are now capable," said they, "of entering the whole blend of the condition induced by the combination of these exercises on which you have been working. You can draw on it any time for sustenance and refreshment, without the continued necessity of an elaborate sequence of specific steps, by the simple device of rising to it. Try to do so in as continuous application as possible in everyday living. Continue the series of steps, as a combined exercise, daily for a short period; also occasionally as separate exercises in review of them as components of that blend, singly and separately. But for the most part regard them as interdependent automatic mechanisms, to be controlled and operated by the orderly subconscious you have trained.

"In discarding—or rather growing out of—the visualized symbols of the abundance idea, you will come to realize that you have not been actually drawing from the abundance of the harvest, or the waterfall, or the power of the sun-warmth, or any of the other symbols we have considered. You have, in reality, by those symbols come in contact with the same sources from which those things themselves draw their vitalities. In other words, you have not taken something from or through them: you have by them been enabled to draw from the same sources from which they draw."

There is all the difference in the world between the man who goes away into his self-made solitude for his own sake, as he conceives it; and him who steps aside into the silences, as the expression goes, to get himself in tune with the infinite and bring back to men a refreshed perception of unity. Don't you see, it is the intention *that makes all the difference. The one expedition into solitude is a self-seeking thing; the other is charged with all the eternal purposes of unity.*

CHAPTER VI

EXCURSIONS

Most of us are practical people, with definite jobs in life, which we want to do efficiently. We have livings to make, and taxes to pay, and businesses to conduct, and people of many kinds to meet and to handle. Desirable as is the "higher life" offered us by various philosophies and systems and cults, much as we should like to enjoy the advantages they offer, we really cannot afford to do so at the expense of our jobs. That attitude may be very ignoble of us, and all that, and we may be low and despicable worms, but the fact remains that our instinct fends us off from anything that is going to make us fuzzy-minded, queer in the eyes of our contemporaries, vague and impractical.

To me that is a natural reaction. I feel that way myself. And I believe it is a legitimate feeling. This is our world: and we are here because we are supposed to live in it and with it. In fact I would even go so far as to say of any system of spiritual development, "If it demands, or causes, withdrawal *in any way*, from hearty human participation in everyday living, depend upon it, it is wrong." That is, it is wrong for us everyday citizens of

137

the world. Saints, holy men—specialists, not general practitioners of life—these may be different: I do not know. But if moving out of the cellar workshop into the upper story is going to result in a skimped and botched product of the workshop, then most of us would prefer to stay below.

With this in mind, I must confess I at first regarded with some skepticism the whole idea of retreat to an inner fortress. It looked to me like just another form of "retiring from the worldly trivialities" in orthodox oriental fashion. What was the difference, after all, between taking yourself off bodily to the Himalayas, and retreating mentally or spiritually to an inner inaccessibility? In either case the part of you that mattered retired from the scene of action.

But there proved to be a distinction which I had missed.

Invisible: You must not think of your inner citadel or core of reality as only a retiring place or refuge. Drawing yourself aside from the common planet because of its disagreeable agitations is no test of that stability. The difficulty in the taking of such shelter is not that it is inefficient, for it is possible to rise to such a consciousness that your skirts are unwet by the storm; but that, when you again stick out your head, the world may have passed you by. Inevitably, if you would progress with the rest, you must take your full share of the buffeting of the elements. The true method, therefore, is to continue in a serene unconcern, knowing well that your inner habitation is secure, but accepting your full share in the common forward movement.

It is only by the buffeting of the storm that men discover their reliances. Those who have not built their habitations, their stability, are then often shaken into an acknowledgment that such habitations are desirable. If the spark is in them, they must begin to search.

While those who have already understandingly constructed a stability have now an opportunity, otherwise lacking, of testing its integrity. Escape, only, is sterile.

This, on the other hand, does not mean that you are called upon to plunge heedlessly into the muck and mire. You must do what is offered to your hand; but it is no more desirable, now, that you cripple your wings by seizing more than your power can lift, than in times of contentment. Do what comes, bear what comes in natural course, but do not overweight beyond what your serenity is capable of floating. Distinguish between withdrawal and hearty but undamaged living.

Storms are a test of your seaworthiness. They are not 'sent as a test,' but come in the usual course of cause and effect. They are times of trial: uncomfortable, distressful, if you have not your own upbearing vehicle of consciousness; stimulating and forwarding of the Scheme, if you have.

Stewart: I still don't understand just when one should use one's inner fortress.

Betty: I am coming out now, and the reality is getting thinner and paler. As I drift away from it, all I can be sure of is that it is not enough just to say with great dignity: I withdraw my consciousness. That is no good. When outside things irritate you, it will work much better if you don't stop at withdrawal—if you complete the circle and come back. If you don't get that, a dignified withdrawal from earth frets looks rather silly!

It was a relief to feel that the Invisibles were on my side. But though honored, I was also a little confused by a dilemma. Apparently the best way to meet disharmony was to retire to your inner fortress. But retirement to your inner fortress stopped your forward progress! A bit paradoxical, it seemed to me. Next day, they straightened me out:

Invisible: This participation in wider consciousness should have a twofold action. It has such endless possibilities that there is always danger to expanding to it until one loses all touch with physical manifestation. Therefore the expansion must always be balanced by the contraction to experiment with material reality. Each thing you expand to; acquire subjectively; you must contract on to make yours objectively, so that you possess it and can utilize it in practical living.

Betty: That's the way I function over here. For instance I expand to an airplane point of view of my own life, to realize that I am in a little room in a chicken-coop house on a tiny speck of the earth's surface, near one of its shores. I see that geographically, as from an airplane.

Then in the little circumambience I am confronted with an amazing conflict, something in the way of resistance to my progress in life. I am to make harmony out of its materials, or else I am to be rended piecemeal, my consciousness made fragmentary by irritations and diminishments, absurd preoccupations with these minutiae. I have that choice always; everybody does. But also I must keep it firmly in mind that my airplane consciousness is no good if I cannot retain it for practical use—not merely for soaring majestically over things and ignoring them, but for bringing the power of a greater vision to bear on the harmonizing of the over-magnified inflamed particles of life.

This is just an illustration to show that expanding to a vision is no good unless you can contract it to your problem, to see if it is yours and if it works. The great danger of all expansion is the lessening of ability to contract purposefully.

Invisible: The point is that symbols of this sort—the airplane one—are useful only when employed for the purpose of interpenetrating your daily lives with the wider consciousness of spiritual reality. It is certainly a great mistake ever to drop your airplane vision altogether, as one is so liable to do when confronted by things one has always done in a certain way. But it is equally a mistake to use it to compartment off earth life completely. Such a course will only cause you to miss your present opportunities and make yourself trouble later.

By all means refine your senses in every possible way. But also practice with them as you would with any other desirable. And remember that the time to practice anything enduring is in the moments of stress. Garnered and gardened peace is only for refreshment, enabling you to return strengthened to your practice hours. It would be ineffectual to eliminate all stress points from your life, for then you would have no experience in *producing* harmony.

Betty: That is the only way we can stabilize our acquisitions—by using them to produce harmony in our lower levels. The process of growth is much like a piston moving up and down in a cylinder, only the upper range is constantly extendible. It moves up to its highest point, and then must return to force down its accretion; because it is impossible for it to go still higher until this lowest range has been compressed into actual manifestation. It can move up, you see, only as it is forced up by the bottom accomplishments.

In the two succeeding interviews the way to go about this was clearly defined. The records of these occasions seem to me so completely satisfactory that I am going to let them stand without comment.

Betty: I'm all cramped up: wait until I get stretched. As soon as I glow steadily, I'll tell you what there is to say.... (A short pause.)

It is about expansion and contraction again. Just now they were showing me how to stretch my muscles and fill my lungs when I get contracted. You lift all the depression and tension and trouble with a motion like stretching from a cramped position and filling your lungs with air after coming out of a house....

You can't lift your trouble with you, though. You've got to leave it in the cramped position you were in. You know it's there, and that you've got to go back to it; but you can go out for a walk.

Invisible: Every time you get stuck or cramped and lose your freedom of action, you should remember about stretching and going outside to fill up with deep breaths and look at something bigger than you are constructing.

(Pause.)

Betty: Now they've brought me back to contemplate my body. They think that I can improve my control....

They're just letting me into my body and out again— just a flash, to get control of doing it. It's wonderful practice in a kind of balance—in keeping my spirit so balanced that it gets no drag from the body....

Invisible: Enter the body....Now release.

Betty: I've got to keep them up; alternating.

Invisible: Try once more.

Betty: Yes, I can do it. Wait until I alternate again....

It's just like magic! With this control I could instantly dematerialize myself so as to be sensitive only to the most delicate vibrations of spirit. And then at a moment's notice I could shift right back to something absolutely external and objective, like a game of tennis. It's just as simple as changing the focus of a microscope to different levels in its depth of field. With this magician's power one could partake of every life that exists....

It is really just a matter of withdrawing your attention from one thing and giving it full strength to another. A moment ago, for instance, I withdrew all attention from my body—left it in the corner and walked off in my spiritual body. It was just as simple as that. I merely withdrew all attention and vitality as one would let down a balloon. And then I repeated it a number of times for practice....

The big lesson in this is that, during the day and about our affairs, we should at intervals practice retiring to our spiritual body and withdrawing attention from the other. It is necessary to keep on doing this until we get control.

Invisible: The ability to separate yourself at will from the entanglements of the minutiae in which you are daily involved, is absolutely essential to the far-seeing control of your destinies. Because efficient accomplishment of any kind demands that you free yourselves periodically to look at your inner relationship to the whole, returning then to apply yourselves to the production of the same harmonious associations without. It is an alternate expansion and contraction, like respiration. If you did not contract with all your strength, you would never produce anything. And if you did not expand with all your strength, you would soon stop producing anything worth while. The great secret of progress is to *alternate* in working out your destinies, as an artist walks away from his picture, and then returns to accomplish it close up.

Betty: Today's message is a crowning thing. It is not something one carries in one's hands; but a vision one sets above. It is the embodiment of aspiration. It's like a great shining door....

Over and over and over again I do it. I bend my head

and sink my mind to infinitesimal examinations of minute laws. And then a great Breath comes over me, and I lift my head and fill my lungs and look up through that shining door. Over and over and over again I alternate thus, until I find that all the life I can take to my minute investigations, which magnifies them and brings comprehension, all the life is in the sustenance I draw from my big breath.

Invisible: You are experiencing the slowed-down movement of all life: how life is refreshed at its source. This is the universal process of creation, of the individual contribution. However rapid or varied, the action is always essentially the same. For constant alternation of the two phases is the only thing that gives ease and facility in precipitation. It is the twofold process of consciousness, of health-maintained existence.

Betty: This isn't just a visionary thing: it's a practical ventilating thing. It's the technique of bringing life to each page you turn in what you are doing. If I only could, I'd show you the process of *all* work in these terms, so that it would be a *practical* impression. It is the *actual process* of all daily work that is the subject today. Don't you see? When minds are concentrated for minute clarifying purposes, the only way to keep them properly vitalized, permeated with spiritual illumination, is by alternating their processes regularly, periodically steeping those same concentrated minds in periods of expansion....

How shall I make that tangible? Somehow I don't feel that the substance I am in is adequately represented by anything I have said....

(Chuckled.)

Very amusing. I was looking at a great big gorgeous world without little confining things. And then I came back and started making a tiny world, like that out there in my garden. And because I've looked at the big

144

one I say: "This won't do; it must have more space and be more like that other one." And I make it more like that other one, without in any way decreasing its productiveness, because I've brought back my inspiration and my proportions and my simplifications.

Invisible: This technique of alternation is an essential part of all spiritual progress, because the first burst of discovery and stimulation, left to itself, tends to wane or have less acquirability. The task then is to take care it doesn't wane, to uphold *mechanically*—it can be done—that first vitalizing fervor which overrides all obstacles and carries you on.

(Pause.)

Betty: I am coming back so curiously. All the glow and passion of conviction oozes back to a lukewarm admission. All the certainty of possibility evaporates to the-best-we-can-do kind of attitude. Oh, dear, I see myself gently laid down, dark and empty and heavy, with only the recollections that you read in the records of the living pulsing gift of life.

Surprisingly few intelligences carry forward steadily with their accepted beliefs in a soldierly fashion, training themselves to be representatives of the force latent in those accepted convictions of their's. It is enough for most people to think a thing out and lay it aside on a top shelf of their minds, occupying themselves with the common exchange articles on the lower shelves. A belief is not a possession unless you demonstrate its workability.

It may all sound very fanciful, but spiritual health demands certain early morning ablutions. These are as vital to the spiritual faculties as the cleanliness with which you prepare the body for its day's activities. Indeed they are far more important, as they also key up and harmonize the body. A little experiment in making a spiritual toilet when you first wake up will prove its great and increasing influence on each day's harmony.

CHAPTER VII

HOMESTEAD

The development of any new country has generally followed a fairly definite routine. First the intrepid explorer in search of adventure and riches. He manages to blunder through by main strength, a combination of luck and natural aptitude. He returns. The story of his discoveries entices others. A certain number of these, also, get there—and back—and the story grows.

Gradually, these first forerunners build up a body of knowledge as to the routes and passes and fords. Thus we reach presently the next stage of development, in which pure adventure becomes secondary to exploitation. Hunters and trappers and miners rove about skimming off the more superficial resources. They have little interest in the country for itself. Their idea is to get what they want in a hurry, and escape home to enjoy it. A certain few may go so far as to establish permanent camps to which they return year after year. But these are not their real headquarters; merely temporary hangouts.

And at the last comes the genuine settler, the homesteader, with his tools and livestock. Only then begins what may be called true development, for these people are cultivators, rather than predators. Their aim is to add something new to the region, rather than to take away something it already has.

With the technique of alternation explained, it now seemed to me that the Invisibles had pretty well covered all the possibilities. I was a good deal like the caterpillar which has eaten all the leaves off his twig, and so believes there are no more leaves in the whole wide world. But I soon found out I was wrong. Not that the Invisibles urged us to further rapid expansion at this time. But in a series of talks they did try to give a glimpse of the direction in which future development might lie.

Betty: I am sitting right on the border today, trying to understand....

Strata....Consciousness is built in layers. When I'm here I'm in the one that rests upon and touches our consciousness. It's just like the water-and-air-level—like being amphibious. Anybody could live half in and half out—both lives. So far I have only come up from the depths temporarily to accustom myself to the different atmosphere of this level above. But what I *want* to do is to live on top, and only occasionally go into the depths....

I wonder why we don't all accustom ourselves to live there? I suppose it is because it seems an unreal world at first. That is because we are still dripping from the depths, and are not dried off and accustomed....

They say they want to show me how consciousness develops into this level above....

(Long pause.)

Can't I go up? I don't see why I have to travel latitudinally....

Curious place, now that I come to look at it. Funny! It looks like a matter of elevations and country and a lot of currents....Why, it's *waves!* There never was such a world of waves before....Seems I'm going to have a lot to do with those waves.

Invisible: Momentary contact, however, brief, with the level above, changes their action.

Betty: That's very interesting. I'll tell him about it.

Invisible: Have him draw it.

(Pause.)

Betty: It's so simple here, yet it takes so many learned people to show me this. I don't see how anything so simple could take such profundity. Very fatiguing to look at such studied things.

(Under direction from the Invisible, Stewart drew the following diagrams:)

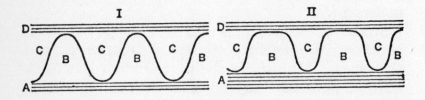

Invisible: "A" represents the field of ordinary human consciousness—call it the static field. "D" is the magnetic field of the higher consciousness. "B, B, B" are the waves of heightened awareness which are continually arising over and across the static field. When this field has attained a certain level of development, these waves at their apexes establish momentary contact

148

with the magnetic field. And as development continues, the interspaces, "C, C, C," gradually diminish, as shown in diagram II, making the points of contact more nearly continuous. When the interspaces are finally eliminated, then the static field is in complete correspondence with the magnetic field, and the individual enters fully the higher consciousness.

(Pause.)

Betty: You know how a motion picture sometimes gets out of frame, and you see half of two pictures at once? Well, that's just the kind of a curious position I am in. All my desire is to establish myself in the upper consciousness. It is so much bigger and I can accomplish so much more in it. It seems to be where I belong. But as the other one gets dimmer I feel a little guilty and bothered about it. I know I'm losing something there, a nice animal thing I almost regret....

Just the same, I think I'll decide to let it go; it can't be helped. I *have* to concentrate on the part I'm interested in, best in, most progressive in. After all, isn't that what you've got to do? Haven't you got to frame up the part of life that most unites you, the best and highest there is in you, and live it with some boldness and decision?

Invisible: The point toward which all this instruction trends is ultimate identification with your higher self. But first must come a vital effort to know that higher self, and a gradual training of your spiritual muscles to maintain it, once recognized.

This does not mean that you should cease to interest yourselves in the multitude of activities all around you—people and books and experiences—these are hourly food. But it does mean most emphatically that your major efforts should be in the recognition and cultivation and establishment of your inner being, the eternal part of you. The gradual growth and expansion

149

of this eternal self is the major business of each day, whatever may be the pressure of obligations in your everyday life.

Betty: Everybody wants *so* much to have us acknowledge this higher consciousness, and not keep it as a kind of bashful idea: to come out and make it respectable as a fact that we are in camp in a new country, and spend all the time we can there. Nothing else seems real to me but just this, and I'm so afraid you're not coming along with me....

No; you're here. But I can't say you are very lively. You are sleeping around camp, and I am the only one who is awake and doing the work.

Betty: In this state of separation from my customary self, I perceive, am aware of a great organization of which I am a part. Some task is being attributed to me, allotted to me. I want and am prepared to do it....

Now a warning is being given as to the process of carrying it out, the point of contact with customary and practical life. It seems to concern the development of my bit of awareness. They say I mustn't cut it off from its supply of growth. Many people take their allotments and let them wither and die. Others take them and force them frantically in an unhealthy growth. The easy, simple, enduring way is to keep your embryonic spiritual being constantly under the rays which nourish it, habitually connected with its main source. It will grow healthfully and naturally and easily that way—if you keep just a ray of its own substance coming through. But taking it and cutting it off kills it, makes many failures, much delay.

Invisible: By the way of general instruction as to future progress, allow us to point out to you the great rule for success in any work of this kind. It is the holding of the form of thought together in simple visualization, the habitual retention of it, and the simple almost trivial experimentation with it. Truly nothing should be considered too small to work on with the tools of eternal values. Their application is to even the most insignificant things, little hourly experiences and situations, the material of a commonplace day, anything pertaining to your life that needs focusing upon.

The alternation for recreation of minds is of course invaluable, but the permanent occupancy of a subject in the mind is what endows it with its greatest power. The laying aside of the higher consciousness for special attention is what retards the personal possession of its attributes. That is usually the trouble: you await great occasion for its use—a crisis, something "worth while." The consequent repeated efforts to re-start are a great waste. It is the momentum of smooth, continuous effort that conserves energy.

Betty: Wait a minute. I perceive the Idea, but I can't concentrate on the fragment before me....

It looks a good deal like shooting. Any dub can make a high score once in a while, but that doesn't mean much. When a marksman wants to see how he's getting along he looks at his *average* score.

Invisible: One acquires a truth as one believes in it, and admits it, and tries to stick to it. Until that truth has become to you an unfailing motive power; until you have established yourself in it without intermission; until you cannot help acting any way but in it; until you are one of its supporting elements, as it were, you do not gain the full benefit of its possession.

It is just so with the higher consciousness. Mostly you do not stick to it. You only sporadically reach up and grasp it, and then drop off and wander about. But the fact remains that as long as you continue satisfied with dropping off, with occasional contacts with it, you remain unplaced and drifting.

This is not to be interpreted as recommending a tight-pressing strangulation hold on the higher consciousness, with the effect of weariness and staleness. The ideal is rather the natural fitting of yourself to it as a recognition of reality you have gradually *surrounded*. Your attitude then becomes a simple natural desire for it in place of recognized inferiorities.

Betty: You see, when I first began to associate myself with this greater harmony, I looked at my tiny perception of it and I said: Certainly there is nothing else I want so much as to feel the security and conviction and satisfied delight within me that comes with that, and to give it to others—to produce it and create it for them. But in the past that has happened only on special occasions. Now I ought to begin to carry that feeling with me ordinarily.

Invisible: The present effort is an attempt to foreshadow the transference of consciousness—the preponderance of consciousness is better—to the spiritual body. In the past this has quite rightly been centered in the earth consciousness, but you are progressing toward a point where your spiritual body will become capable of taking over the direction of the parent or earth self. When this is attained it will be roughly as if your earth life were in the balloon basket of a great buoyancy. From this inexhaustible, indestructible higher buoyancy sinews of strength will support the core of your ordinary experience. It is in such companionable association with spiritual values that one develops a conviction of the reality of these finer potentialities, and gradually learns to sense and utilize the power existent in them. Then, instead of being in leaden contact with the earth, submitting to its influence and its unilluminated lower laws, one is magnetically liberated and in the controlled power of a different specific gravity.

Betty: Suppose we turn the tables tonight, and I ask you to define what has been said of this process. Then we'll tackle the weak spots.

Stewart: (Made a stab at giving his conception of habitual spiritual consciousness.)

Betty: Yes. That's all quite right. But don't forget that what you have just described is a more or less remote goal; and that the technique best suited to us at present is more elementary than that.

The very first thing always is the tuning of yourself, your leap or levitation of heart to your Source—the absolute tuning of yourself. You are then imbedded in something so much more potent than yourself, so incomprehensibly secure that all you can do is to sense the comfort of it, lend yourself rapturously to it.

Next, while you are competely comfortable, composed and warmed and reassured of your divinity—while you are there, before any tensions can start, while power is upon you—decide what you are going to do when you are farther away from it; when you have changed your focus. Then proceed wholeheartedly to use your ordinary faculties in clean-cut application to the thing in hand.

What I am trying to say is: don't mix up your regions of consciousness. Keep your compartments organized so you can step from one to the other with no fuzzy places between. When occupied with something practical, don't keep wondering if you are working in a spiritual way. It is not necessary to be continually hurrying back to reassure yourself of the spiritual quality. The Source will not desert you until you yourself deliberately shut it out—until you lose your surety

153

and strangle yourself with tensions.

Only one important thing has to be watched: the sensing how long you can work masterfully without renewing yourself. It is your individual rhythm that determines this, and there is nothing difficult about it: just do not go on working when you feel that depreciation has set in. Then a momentary return to attunement is all that is necessary; *provided*, of course, you have made a strong and accustomed home of it.

Stewart: But how about this business of establishing your permanent home so completely that you will be able to do your work directly from it as your headquarters?

Betty: That holds good, of course, in the long run; but right now I am trying to set down a kindergarten way for practical use with our present limited earth consciousness. And the two outstanding points of it are: to spend always plenty of time tuning yourself in comfort at your Source, plenty of time to have it well established; and then never to doubt that it follows you when your mind is completely freed from it in the minutiae of work.

It is a technique that stays with us when we are not illumined and tuned — in the rough-and-tumble of things. I am trying to get something clear-cut for the rough-and-tumble. You are apt to send out then a sort of desperate feeler for something you think you have lost. You feel that you ought to be doing something different and extra-special about something you have left behind you. I want to do away with that. If you are running a car at high speed you can't afford to look up rapturously for inspiration. You've got to trust that the stars are still here, and that you can look up to them when the night comes.

Spiritual impetus should be just as practical as a hot-water faucet or an electric light—and just as available at any moment for efficient action. It is *not* a thing we have to go apart to seek, though it is absolutely dependent on our previously having gone apart to seek. The emphasis in nearly all spiritual instruction is on the going apart to seek, and the technique of the next sequence, the creative use of it, is often left out.

Invisible: It is most important that you do not get a misconception of what we intend to convey by the term "habitual spiritual consciousness." This does not imply any retirement into some state of permanent abstraction, nor any priggish watchfulness to determine that your every move is transcendental. It means simply that each day, when you finish your practice, you do not close the experience like a book, but carry it around with you like a treasured possession. Instead of being completely forgotten, it remains in the back of your mind, communicating its influence automatically to your actions and reactions, and ready at any moment, if specifically called upon, to lend a helping hand.

It is particularly necessary, perhaps, to distinguish this state clearly from the periods of intense concentration you employ for training and development. In especial exercises such as these, you are for a purpose temporarily focusing on certain aspects of yourself. During these periods you impose on the other aspects your command that they sit still and do not bother you, so to speak, until you have finished. You totally—or as nearly so as possible—inhibit their activities. You dismiss all reports from the subconscious: you clear the conscious mind of thought.

But when you invoke the higher consciousness in the course of normal daily living you do not do this. The bodily functions then proceed with no less, and no more, than your customary awareness of them. Your brain-mind moves forward on an unintermitting stream of thoughts and mental images. A bodily or mental vacuum is unnatural and impossible. To check the flow of these things is also unnatural, and allowable only for a special purpose. Whole living implies the simultaneous functioning of all the parts of yourself. Only the sharp focus of your attention is shifted as desired to that portion of your being where it is important that it should function for the business of the moment.

You must at all times remember, however, that it is as serious a mistake to concentrate wholly in the superconscious as it is in the brain-mind or the body. To each its balanced due of yourself; for the balancing is the art of life. The ascetic is no more praiseworthy than the sensualist, and the sensualist is no more to be blamed than is the ascetic. And the pure intellectualist is no more admirable—or deplorable—than either.

Betty: (After a pause.) It's beautiful. They said right away that today was to be a culmination, but they've got me so expanded I can't contract on words. There's some very beautiful language prepared, though, if I could only get it. It swirls around me....

Invisible: Consider carefully a cross-section of each day as you have lived it, like an apple cut across, making visible its core and the seeds maturing within: so examine your own heart and its activities, *one day at a time*. What was your principal aim this day? In the midst of your temporary activities, what percentage of your best energy do you find consciously directed toward an enduring pursuit? In other words, taking this day as a fair example and adding to it *a few hundred similar ones*, what would you say you had created? What sort of a person have you built for yourself? Do you approve of your habitual consciousness?

156

Now take the future, and examine in like manner the allotments of vitality you plan to distribute during your days. Regarding your thoughts and acts as charges of energy with definite amperage and voltage, consider which of these impetuses you intend to continue on persistently, as worthy of a distant aim. Plan to accomplish those first; they are your permanent structure. Then whatever is left of energy charges determine to utilize generously, even to the tiny ones which make gay and humorous sparks enlivening all human intercourse.

Finally, at intervals during each day stop for a moment to rate the percentages of attention and ardor you are actually putting into your various affairs. Examine these percentages as if they were an allotment of finances in a business budget. Then step aside from them a moment, return to the concept of your business of eternal purposes, and compare the two. At length, put them together, asking yourself which ones of these ordinary activities you can so vitalize that they help you to unite with other lives in greater inclusion of the consciousness which we are striving to make for you an everyday affair. (Long pause.)

Betty: I've been trying to make a certain map of my life—to put my interests on different grades, major and minor, and lots in between. I've just been looking my life over quickly to see how to go about it....

To start with, everything was of almost equal importance because of newness and adventureness. Then some were more attractive to repeat than others. Thus I got my contours—by selecting those that had abiding interest for me. They came up like high ridges. And then I used all the other little things as amusements and refreshments and embellishments. They are not at all conflicting or distracting. They just naturally adjust themselves according to your capacity, and

157

enrich your application to your specialities....

Invisible: The suggestion we are trying to present is that you learn to construct your days on a plan of more varied planes, more in keeping with the country you are now traversing. Let the height, the embodiment of your directing beliefs, be the mountains, the main shaping course of your travels, visible always through every occupation and in every chart of your course. Let your daily pursuits, all the lesser allegiances of your mind, be on the water level, fluid, adaptible to the expedience of the stronger structure. Shape your days mentally always thus in contour, never monotonously, jumblingly lacking in distinctions of structure. Waking in the mornings, review the day from your heights, always impregnably establishing your directions from them; returning to them at hours of the day made habitual. From the mountain top you know where the valley leads and what is beyond, and so can plan your movements in the lowlands.

Betty: Now I know what to do when I get down there: I'm going to shut my eyes frequently for the purpose of strengthening my vision of where I'm heading. I don't care how crowded and narrow and circuitous it is, I'm going to remember to live up there and just do business at the bottom.

Invisible: Only thus, persistently practiced, can you avoid the deplorable banality of flattening your life and entering your next existence unmodelled and unbeautiful, without possession of either tools or design. Your potentialities are visible, the rising and falling of your efforts, the acquisition of much that is nebulous; but the firmly made structure itself is only worked out in daily contours. For however developed and exalted your aims may be, they are only nebulous until you give them perpetuating form in your hourly life visible to others.

This is the awakening ceremony I advise for the entire remainder of your life on earth. Its importance is impossible for you to calculate. Its participation, gradually, earnestly, and interestedly, will, without anything but pleasurable effort, bring you inestimable happiness and power.

One hears it so often said that the subject of psychic ex-
ploration interferes with normal living. That is absurd.
Little knowledge misunderstood and misapplied might in-
hibit the adjustment to ordinary environment; but that is
the awkward stage of the neophyte.

I see a drab-colored duty-person wearisomely doing
good, doing right; and then there's a cheerful, comfortable
selfish person doing things enthusiastically that don't do
anybody much good. He has a vital spark: the other hasn't.
That is the reason the selfish person appears to get on so
well: he has the vital spark of being united.
It's more important than we realize—this ingredient of
eagerness. It is the difference between being magnetized
and unmagnetized. Take that cheerful, selfish person who
does things enthusiastically: he has started by getting at
least a harmony of two ingredients. He is doing from the
fact that he wants to do it—he has got two of his ingredi-
ents. The other has only one: he is doing, but he does not
want to do it. He is pulling the other way inside, so it's
only half.

CHAPTER VIII

EASY STAGES

Every teacher of anything that demands skill and
training knows that the average beginner always wants
to get somewhere in a hurry, and is impatient of the
slightest delay. And that when he begins to get some
idea of what he is really up against, he probably does
one of two things: he groans despairfully and sits down
where he is; or he turns on the pressure, and tries to
burn up the road. The eventual result in either case is a
full stop.

This is especially true of our present subject. The
ideal of habitual spiritual consciousness is one that

reacts on people most definitely. It either frightens a man away altogether; or it inspires him to over-zeal. That is natural. When he has come thus far, he is able to see that it is not only an important job, but also a tremendously formidable job. It offers either a supreme prize or a great burden.

However, it will be a great burden only if we try to take its whole weight at once. After all, big jobs are never done thus. As children we did not take up life that way. We played with our toes, and waved our legs, and managed to roll over, and got on our hands and knees and crawled, and shortly succeeded to a very wobbly perpendicular. We did what we could at the moment. Furthermore we did it because we wanted to, and because we enjoyed it. We had an impulse to walk and run, but there was no burdensome pressure of compulsion that we should do so right now. And most certainly no damaging of our present joy in life because we were not doing so. Ultimates were unknown to us, and so there was no danger whatever of our adopting ends as immediate obligations.

The Invisibles repeatedly reminded us of this. We had become aware of new functions and possibilities in ourselves, they admitted; but mere awareness did not imply that something tremendous was required of us. No child-labor was expected. We were permitted time to discover and develop these new faculties, just as physical life had permitted us time to discover and develop our physical faculties.

"Spiritual development," said they, "is not a desperate struggle for anything. In fact it is absolutely the contrary. It is a secure embryonic stirring, a happy stretching into one's own peculiar universe, a basking in growth sensations until one establishes oneself in permanent strength. It is not a strain, nor an obligation to assume anything you do not absolutely possess. It is a great and quiet letting in of something that is already there. You just surround what is yours—move into it. Between these two there is a great difference. One defeats the purpose; the other co-operates. One is a kind of warm hospitality which fosters growth; the other is a strain and sterility and affectation of the over-zealous.

"Your watchword must be never to allow any strain to enter into the practice of your individual expansion or spiritual flame feeding. Of course, every now and then this system is bound to go wrong, and you will get to pressing and cramping on life, straining it through your own dusty self instead of just admitting it as through an open window. But that is all wrong, nevertheless. Spiritual development is never a straining up of any kind after something to be grasped by force."

No matter what his line of endeavor, every man sooner or later learns to admit the value of taking it easy. A few even go so far as a sincere effort to infuse the idea, as a general principle, into their active lives. But applying it to the particular instance is always another matter. High pressure in any special case is only too easy to rationalize and justify. Quite often we do not even recognize it as high pressure. We have always done things that way.

Ordinary affairs of life often let us off without too much penalty. They allow us to muddle through somehow by main strength and awkwardness. In one way or another we get by without too much friction. But this journey into the high country of consciousness is a more serious matter. We cannot speed on this narrow trail and stay on it.

Fortunately we have one simple and reliable test of our position to which at any time we can refer to ourselves. That is our state of mind. By and large, leaving aside the small mosquito-annoyances, if we are not having a peaceful, carefree, normal time on our way, count on it, we are headed for the swamp. Nervousness and depression and depletion, or exaltation and elation and extravagance: these should alike be recognized as danger signals. First aid is to take off the pressure.

Such things seem very simple in the telling, but curiously enough, they are hard to keep in mind. The ways we can run off into the mud are so many; and the reasons why we did so are so good! Yet in every instance the application of this one test and this one remedy would have prevented all the trouble. But we simply do not remember!

It is interesting to look back through the records and see how carefully the Invisibles guided us in this. Whenever over-intensity threatened, they were always ready with the necessary antidote. Usually they merely laughed at us or cracked foolish jokes. More rarely they went into the matter more seriously; like this:

Betty: There is such a cheerful, exhilarating, lighthearted influence around me today. There isn't going to be anything heavy or philosophical. It is more on the profound wisdom of lightheartedness....

You see, this is the idea: the supreme wonder of recent unfoldments, the fixing of the vision of the road ahead, has given vitality and direction to our steps, but also it has necessarily taken a somewhat sober trend. This is no cause for worry unless it leads to fixation. At first all of us have a certain awkwardness of spiritual gait; it is a form of the self-consciousness that is not yet mastery.

Invisible: Long ago we gave certain vitally important warnings of dangerous symptoms invariably connected with spiritual progress. You remember the "humility and negations" of the godly, the necessity of vitality for spiritual thought. You remember the fluidity, flexibility, to be preserved, the danger of crystallization. This is one of the most important of the definite warnings that can be given. In the beginning the tendency is always to interpret in terms of your bodily functions. Because the body has to contract its muscles to reach out and pick up anything, you contract and strain over your acquisitions of the spirit, making them heavy-duty. It should be the other way around. By applying spiritual principles and methods to your physical activities, you should re-educate the body to greater freedom and flexibility.

Betty: What we need now is a lot of free sports and exercise, carrying the same bigness and expansion into our earth responses that we use in directing our spiritual steps to their goal. All the gateways of the senses must be as wide as the gateway of the inner vision. It's hard to say, because this directing of the vision sideways, as it were, instead of straight ahead must be a spontaneous enjoyment, and not another sober effort.

Invisible: What we are trying to do is to indicate a method of overcoming spiritual awkwardness. To put it roughly, the contagion of youthful beauty of body, loveable, universally adored, must somehow be translated into your spiritual youth. It needs more "puppiness" on your part, more careless play with its sensations. The development of the higher perceptions brings to you sympathy and understanding and compassion, but also at first a somewhat amateurish handling of life. The only way to strengthen and be comfortable and assured in these higher faculties is secretly to romp in them, humorously to perceive that you are rather flat-footed in them. For example, however absurd in some aspects this may appear, however unaccustomed and ridiculous, try momentarily to enter the sensation, recall the childhood memories of progressing light-footedly, the skipping just above that gravitation-weight which comes later in life. (Pause.)

Betty: I'm having such a good time! I'm just skipping and tripping along the top of the Sierra Nevada. The sky is deep blue—and it's such a nice touchable sky! I can swirl the glistening snow around, and feel the sting of its warmth. I've got such unbreathed air, too. It is pure life, containing all substance—new and exciting. I like having access to high peaks. I love that warm sun and blue sky and crisp snow....

And now I am pacing shining sands in the full strength of a runner. There is no effort to it at all, and the sands are hard and fresh-scoured by the drained-off waters. The air is all glinting, too, and quickened with purity. It hasn't had dust thrown in it yet.

I've got to leave it now....

Invisible: If occasionally you could play some such game of light-footedness, it would be the greatest possible technique of comfort in continuing your spiritual progress. You must not deny your rainbow soul its playtime. If you only realized what wings grow during this playtime, and how glad you would be to have them!

Betty: The whole thing is to prance more when you find yourself becoming super-solemn. It's tremendously important, because almost everyone in our stage of development falls into the danger of utilizing his expansion straight ahead alone, instead of also sideways and circularly. That doesn't mean we should abandon our forward-reaching consciousness and enter a world of mere pleasure and vapidity. But we must cultivate our enjoyments and hobbies and enthusiasms: they safeguard the ease and grace of our true direction.

Always remember there's a twofold dimension to it: perpendicular and horizontal.

At first, as might be expected, we did not fully appre-

165

ciate the seriousness of this danger or the importance of its antidote. In those days we were so busy getting our aim straight and trying to follow the right trail, that we spared little attention for such apparently unimportant details as speed of travel. Consequently, when the translation slowed down or the intake seemed blocked or we otherwise encountered what the records term "difficulty"—we followed the natural impulse to re-double the pressure and work twice as often and twice as long. As a result, things always went from bad to worse, until finally Betty went on a temporary strike and refused to do anything more at all.

But gradually we learned that high-pressuring our-selves into eternity was no good—not in any circum-stances whatever. It is easy to say "we learned"; but, please believe me, take-it-easy is something that re-quires a whole lot of learning! And even when, at long last, we were thoroughly convinced, we still had to rec-ognize when we were actually breaking step.

One traditional speeding-up method which has led many astray is asceticism. In days of old, all serious as-pirants thought it necessary to beat and starve and otherwise torment themselves in order to subdue the "vile body." That idea even today carries some weight. There are still people who wear hair shirts and lie on beds of nails with a view to "acquiring merit." Some sects even go so far as to believe that suffering is the only direct road to development.

From the start a healthy instinct warned us against this sort of thing. Its crude and obvious form repelled us; but before long we discovered that it had a way of presenting itself in disguise. Unexpectedly we would find ourselves floundering in a patch of extremely prickly brush, and wondering how we got there. Occa-sionally, when it seemed important, we would be shooed away in this fashion:

166

Betty: Today I have been sensitized to get into the crow's nest, as it were, to see what a lookout can call down to you. And the thing that I pick up as being especially to be said is the sensation I get of ourselves physically. It is one of regretting the loss of something valuable and enjoyable and necessary to a whole being. Too high a price has been paid physically for what has been attained spiritually.

Invisible: Always in the earlier years of spiritual development the effort of stilling your objective minds to reach your inner ones has certain accompanying symptoms which result in a flattening and dulling of the entity as a whole. It is just as when, in a sport, one uses undue effort in the beginning and exhausts oneself in doing what later can be done quite easily. The aching muscles of the mind and spirit sometimes interpret themselves in reflex even on the bodily muscles. A curiously ageing effect is produced, co-existing with the moments of increased vitality and spiritual exuberance.

To overcome this interaction the body must be made as robust as possible. Sometimes the flattening and dulling of it comes through various misinterpretations of the relation between the spiritual and the physical. For instance, the growth in refinement of the inner being may interpret itself into anemia of the physical being—into restrictions of foods and appetites of all kinds. Actually no such negations interact favorably on the higher centers. That sounds like a dangerous doctrine, but in reality the danger is more apt to occur on the side of damaging the spontaneity of the body's functions—its buoyancy and equilibrium and youthful confidence and carelessness. Only too easily the aspirations of the inner life misinterpret themselves into such restrictions as an overregulated child would suffer.

167

You can prove this to yourself by experiment. On occasion try deliberately breaking over any hard and fast rules you may have made for yourself physically, and observe the reflex of comfort and fluidity your whole being will enjoy. Men of genius have almost always had a keen, though often an unbalanced appreciation of this. The wide-flung liberties, amounting at times to license, of many poets in their physical lives have reacted in great boldness and liberation of spirit. This is not to be recommended, of course, for there is grave danger in such wide unrhythmic swoops, great ultimate loss of balance. However, the principle involved is here clearly seen.

Stewart: You do not agree, then, with those who believe there is great power in such things as total abstinence from sex expression?

Invisible: What good is there in total abstinence?

Stewart: Why, to escape control by one's lower nature, I suppose.

Invisible: You should not be controlled by anything. But total abstinence merely means that you are controlled by fear of it. In either case you are controlled by it.

The peculiar characteristic of the present age in contrast to that which has developed past mystics is the jovial, healthful naturalness which it is to demonstrate. Spiritual consciousness is to be, not a laboratory experiment under conditions painfully devised, but a world-wide possession thrust into the life of a new and vital race of people. There is no longer any need to accept the conditions under which former contemplations were obliged to function. It is to be the free swing of the athlete, and not the labored tread of the weary monk.

Individuals vary much in the need for this warning, but again I want to state that spiritually and physically whatever you do translates and reacts in each medium. They should be comfortably interacting, interlocked. Therefore any grace and freedom and lack of restraint in one liberates the other. You want buoyancy and equilibrium in each, aiding the other. Breathe deeply and freely in *both*, and be on guard against stiffening regulations if you value your flexibility and comfort.

Above all, do not let your body lose its toe-dancing ability, do not too long let it become stagnant, even for many hours at a time, during these years of development. Keep red blood and good food and raw air constantly active through it in any happy-go-lucky, unregulated flexible ways you can devise. All loss of this or stiffening of its habits will result in precisely the same thing spiritually. You cannot possibly get into a natural normal spiritual life, an habitual consciousness of it, unless you recreate a childhood attitude of body, without any Prussianizing "mature" restrictions.

PART THREE
USE

You don't really own a thing unless you use it. You can have titles of possession, but they are only scraps of paper. Can't you imagine a man who doesn't know how to read, owning a library with every book in the world in it. All he owned would be stuff. He couldn't eat it. He couldn't get anything out of it!

How do you benefit from your body? Not by just possessing it. You exercise it! And it is just the same with the higher consciousness. It's worth nothing to you, or anybody else, unless you use it.

Desire to receive is but half the span of the bridge. Visualize this as the exact condition of your present spiritual progress. You have constructed but half the span of the bridge. Without the completion of this work you will have but struggled in vain; because the reason for its being is that, when finished, something may pass over it from the free field of spiritual perception to the congested consciousness of the world.

The mere desire to receive, alone, is not sufficient even to establish effective contact with the informing intelligence above yours. In fact, it has a great difficulty to be overcome in what might be called a suctional *quality, which precipitates the force above it, reduces it to a lower manifestation in which it no longer functions as a quickening inspirational force. It becomes merely an intellectual 'record'—not a gift of growth silently available through you to others.*

CHAPTER I

PRODUCTION

A good analogy is a most helpful device, as we know, in clarifying our understanding. But a true analogy is better than that. It may be followed with confidence. The reason for this is that a "true analogy is merely the same law working in different mediums," as the Invisibles expressed it.

This truth was of enormous help to us. We had spent most of our lives poking about into odd corners of the world, "exploring," "pioneering." We knew that game: and how to go at it, and how to keep out of trouble, and to take care of ourselves when thrown on our own. So when we started out on this new type of exploration in the frontiers of consciousness, we—largely as a matter of habit—used the same methods of approach. They worked. So, with increasing assurance, we fell into our familiar wilderness techniques. They were effective; and they continued to be effective even in the later advanced stages of instruction and experiment.

Now after a man has, by his vision and his woodcraft, penetrated to a country new to him, and wants to stay awhile, the first thing he must do is to clear a space for himself, and on it construct a habitation, a shelter against the elements and a safe defense against predatory beasts. Next he must assure his warmth, his food, and his drink. These are essential for survival.

But once he has them, he will next want to "improve his lot," as he calls it. He must establish relationships with neighbors, however few and distant they may be. And these relationships—if his "lot" is to improve— depend on one thing. Production. The more he produces, the more he has to share; and the more, therefore, he will receive back. And the reverse must be true. If he produces less, he will have less to share. Or to pay with, if you care to express it that way.

This was precisely the situation to which we had now attained. We had found our country; we had made ourselves a place in it; we had built our defense. We could survive. But if we were to make anything out of the achievement, we could not merely sit down in our stockade and think about it. There was more to it than just that.

There is still another way in which the analogy carries on perfectly. Traveling any remote region is always hard going. There are not detailed maps nor paved roads. The pioneer must expect to work at it harder than he ever had to work back in that comfortable country whence he came. We are exactly in the same case

174

here, at this point of our journey together. What follows is not going to be easy reading. That is because it deals with another of those subjects which must be actually experienced before it can be completely understood. Only part of it can be conveyed in words.

The foregoing statement is intended to be an incentive and not a discouragement. Understanding by both words and experience is a fumbling sort of thing, baffling as a difficult game; but, also like a game, it is fun. We can say this with authority, for we too went through the groping in fog and mist, picking up a piece here and a piece there until we had collected our comprehension. Rarely, indeed, did the Invisibles go at any new subject directly. They darted at it; pecked at it, so to speak, touching it in brief guerrilla raids of hint and half-statement, until our minds were prepared for discourse. Possibly that system might be better in presentation here; but space forbids. We must do our best with selected discourses, and trust to the reader's interest and good will to supply the missing ingredient. If he will be content to remain undiscouraged by initial— and necessary—vagueness; if he will keep faith that the vagueness is only a mist through which but a few steps in experience will bring him into sunlight, he will eventually return to the stockade—to finish the analogy— with spoils rich in substance.

Let us, then, start out on our quest through one of Betty's symbolic experiences.

Betty: What do you suppose that commonplace little city is? There is a remarkable story about it—about someone in it who has achieved great freedom. Quite a story....

If I were to tell it to you, I would have first to make a picture of very commonplace drab ugliness; a little cheap room in a dismal boarding house in a miserable sort of town. It smells dirty and dusty. It is a dirty, dis-

175

piriting, hopeless, carpetty, spotty, ugly-proportioned place in a cindery and smutty horrid little town. This man who lives there is feeding his soul on beauty; riotous, gorgeous beauty; beauty that is full of life and lavishness. He comes over here for it. He has found out how.

It would make a delicious thing to write. First I would get just suffocated with grimy windows and dirty carpets and unwashed paint and dusty lace curtains. I'd get black and beauty-dead. And then, after I'd taken time to get words that would bring that smell to your nostrils, *then* I'd have a good time! Then I would have everything blended and gorgeous in depths of tones; and I'd have the flash and sparkle of response to the fleeting life that comes in sun and dewdrops and glistening petals and evanescent things whose preciousness is in just the moment of sight—not in registered values, like gems. I'd just wallow in that stuff, making word-refreshments. Amethyst colors would be there—amethyst and amber, that's a nice combination; and the deep, deep shadows making the richness, and the splashes of light on top; and the perfumes occupying all space like the sunrise. It is beauty like that I'd chase, until my own expanding heart and beating throbbing aroused circulation and radiation of warm life was to me the greatest beauty and reality of all....

(Pause.)

I just happened to meet this man I've been telling you about, and he showed me his garden of riotous beauty. I was enjoying it tremendously; but suddenly something troubled me that does not bother him at all. It is this: I can't just come and wallow in this gorgeousness, and then lead the sort of after-the-jag life he does in his dirty smelly world. It would not be fitting to a sojourner in that country. This man is away ahead of me in abandon to it, but he is not connected up....

176

How can I connect up that dirty plush world with the amethyst and amber one? There they both are: one as real as the other. The world we are in now is just for the purpose of discovering how to lift the one to the other. Can't you see? *You've got to combine them.*

(Pause.)

There! I've had the man go out, and I've eliminated all that dirty stuff from the room, and torn up the carpet and thrown out all that awful old furniture—hot soapsuds!—and I've painted it all over with nice fresh paint. That's the sordid facing of things as they actually are. It must be done. Can't overlook that, while you live here. It's quite a nice little room now, and it brings it that much nearer to the garden of riotous beauty.

Now I can bring in a few beautiful things; maybe a few flowers or a little beautiful-shaped thing. It is so much more comfortable because I've brought them nearer together.

Here is the point. You are never entitled to play in a garden like that—you really aren't—unless you keep on trying somehow to lift your own world a little nearer to it.

Invisible: Spiritual development must always be a twofold effort. Along with the continual onward-upward movement, pressing back boundaries, must go the sympathetic spreading of the perception you have acquired. You must be conquering, overcoming the world with it: giving what you have in such a way that it will enter others and start similar action.

In fact, there is little permanent value in having learned to use the higher laws unless you can do this. Suppose with their help you have succeeded in transmuting an area around yourself—have made a start at surrounding yourself with harmony and health and happiness. Still you haven't really accomplished much unless you can maintain the effectiveness of your perception by spreading it. That area, that transmutation, must spread, expand around you, or you will find yourself possessed only of narrow puritanical piety.

(Pause.)

Betty: How curious! First it was only a continuous upward line. Then a horizontal line somehow joined it and made a cross....

Oh, I see! What a wonderful symbol of the twofold action!

(At this point, under direction from the Invisibles Stewart drew the following diagrams:)

Invisible: Figure I illustrates the upward-reaching element of spiritual contact and growth, supported on a shaft of daily accomplishment in ordinary living. Figure II shows the spreading on your own level of the perception you have attained. To complete the picture it should be imagined that as each level is fulfilled the cross-arm moves upward to represent the next level, the cross meanwhile always keeping the same proportion. In other words, when the level is raised, the upper part of the vertical shaft reaches a little higher into the unknown and the lower end is lost or absorbed.

As a general symbol of individual development this will bear study, but the point we wish to emphasize now is that the higher consciousness is essentially a co-operative affair, not a single independent thing. No matter how simplified your awareness of it may become, how clear your aim or your comprehension of what you are after or how devoutly you may follow it, it does not work effectively unless you have a sympathetic comprehension of the interrelation. Otherwise there is always some kind of drag of the whole on you, no matter how hard and fast you try to travel.

Betty: I feel it curiously as though I were in a line with something. I can go on individually, I can go beyond it; and yet I am so closely related. It is like pressing my breast against a harness that unites us all. I am only successful as I comprehend that unity. I seem to be free, gloriously free; I can go as far as I want by my own energy, volition, desire and enthusiasm: and yet when I pause a moment in that onward push, I am so conscious of this breast harness by which I push the whole with me.

Then there is that other aspect of it. Each person I help to the consciousness of taking his place seems to lighten the drag of the whole against me. Not each person that I help: each person that *is* helped to take his place. So naturally it follows that it is only common sense to try to lessen the drag as you go along by lending a hand to others. It is the only intelligent way.

We were at this time groping our way very cautiously, not only searching new ground for our feet, but testing each step carefully. Especially did we feel that we must examine critically every statement that seemed to bear relationship with conventional cliches. One of these cliches was embodied—to us at least—in the word "service." That word admittedly expresses a profound truth; but often it merely means following the line of least mental resistance. It has been terribly tarnished by the multitudinous zealots who make of it an excuse for holier-than-thou exhibitionism, for meddling, for smug proselytizing, and for neglecting the home fires in favor of wholesale annoyances. There

179

is a certain presumption in setting oneself up as so much more qualified than one's fellows; and to Simple Souls, like ourselves, this job that had been handed us looked big enough. Just pushing toward the higher consciousness seemed a sufficient lifework.

But the Invisibles did not intend us to remain long in that attitude of mind.

Invisible: We do not want to risk having what has been taught slip into the mistaken self-aggrandizement which claims a superlative power, but which is concentrated merely on one's own magnification of individual power. In past ages a withholding of the laws of the higher consciousness has been necessitated through just such a misapprehension. Actually, habitual spiritual consciousness is never an aggrandizement of individual power, although that conception is at present enjoying a very elaborate popular exposition. Brought down to an everyday workable attitude of mind, it is more an aggrandizement of humanity....

Betty: This is very difficult. Language is gone: I am pursuing the idea, but it hasn't any clothes.

(Pause.)

Invisible: Let us begin again.

What is habitual spiritual consciousness? As applied to oneself, it is the placing of oneself permanently on the frontier of one's highest reaches of perception. However often we may fail to maintain the position, it is a definite attempt and a wholehearted possessing desire to live to the fullest of one's capacity in spiritual perception by means of those methods you have written down.

But the mere maintaining of a single example of harmony oneself is only half. The stopping of the idea there would in the long run result in mere loneliness and bafflement. For whatever individual satisfaction this may supply privately in moments of harmonious

180

adjustment, the treasure which you have gathered about you eventually becomes useless, like miser's gold, unless you share its value with the world.

Look for a moment at the usual misapplication of the higher consciousness. A little nugget of spiritual substance is captured by some mind and hoarded. Separated from its own source of life, sealed up in human selfishness, it begins at once to deteriorate. And that is the important thing to realize: this unified consciousness cannot be imprisoned and shackled. Every glimpse of it you get must be felt in its life movement. It must be held lightly and loaned to others, passed freely and lavishly. One's function is to *help conduct a flow*—not to steal a cupful of something and run away with it.

Betty: That is what I have to do, now that I've learned to move my consciousness up: I've got to turn on the current after I've made the connection.

Invisible: Add to this the idea that from now on *your outgo must equal your intake.* You are rapidly outgrowing the stage where you contain as a quiet pool, a backwater, a portion of the current of life. In future your status must be one of continuous movement, without stoppage in your point of contact with the world. Obstruction is there at present.

Betty: I've been so busy getting this thing into my consciousness, and now I've got to be just as busy getting it out—and it's just as hard. After getting it into you there is just as much difficulty and obstruction in letting it out!

Invisible: The action of the earth consciousness is constantly toward closing channels after they have been opened. You get hurt some time, and then you seal off that avenue. You don't succeed somewhere, and you stop trying in that direction. You pretend you do not like and do not want something you cannot

181

have. Thus commonplace living becomes a progressive sealing off of channels that should be free-flowing. The effect is similar to that of closing bodily pores or stopping bodily circulation. It is the pursuit of this course that has thrown the world into its present diseased condition.

Remember, always, that the first point of health is the active, life-creating property that comes from constant inflowing and outflowing. Something of the secret of intake is yours, but you must not forget to be *constantly giving out.*

(Pause, during which a wood thrush began singing outside.)

Betty: That is what they mean: that bird. His best— plus his response from the universal.

(The thrush kept on singing, repeating his liquid musical phrase persistently, over and over.)

Betty: He is still doing it. He isn't filled up yet. You see, he fills up, magnetically, by giving out. That is the way creatures get their life force. A frog croaks, and gets his that way. People get some of it when they laugh or sing together.

The higher consciousness as a *current;* not a pool of still waters. A flow through; not merely an immersion in. We had, unconsciously, fallen into the habit of thinking of it as a kind of private bathtub; and that all we had to do was to cultivate Betty's "receptivity" to become all plumped up and saturated with spiritual grace.

That was a most limiting idea. For one thing, it implied that the amount we could receive, or appropriate, was determined by the size of the container we had made of ourselves; and once we were full-up we were full-up, and that's all there was to it, and the inflow

182

stopped. But this new conception of *something that flowed* through changed all that. The way to make room for more was to use more. And, further, draining out for use established suction for the flowing in. Our output would be actually the measure of our intake. Why, it was almost mathematical! The limit disappeared. There was no limit!

In the enthusiasm of this illumination we overlooked the fact that the strength of the hose does have something to do with how much pressure you can force into it, and therefore with how much water can pass through it. But that came later. At the moment we were delighted at discovering what seemed to be a definite mathematical basis for "service." The word was brightened up for us. Instead of a vague ethical "duty," it began to look like what amounted to a clear-cut scientific necessity.

Before long they elaborated the idea still further.

Betty: I am in the reality of the higher consciousness, but I can't get any relation with the philosophy. Make an outline.

Stewart: We have dealt with the subject of intake and stabilization. Now we must deal with the outgo.

Betty: Yes, that's it. You see, we are apt to think of this connective mind as something one retires into quietly, with plenty of time and great effort. But that is only the passive phase of it. The active phase is what I am coming into now, the utilizing of the connective mind in the world of affairs.

Invisible: It is an infiltration of your bit of universal substance into what is below you. Up to now you have been busy going the other way, but the time has come when you must begin acting below in order to get the power to dart above.

What shall we call this incursion into your lower element? It is a sort of down-thrust after the upward ex-

183

tension—a definite *movement* in return. Whatever you practice hereafter, keep in mind the strong downthrust as necessary for rebound.

(Pause.)

Betty: This is difficult. No more inspiration poured in. I am up against a curious kind of waiting for some *acts* of mine. I see that clearly, but can't seem to make the effort.

Invisible: The hoarding of spiritual perception is extremely difficult to overcome. It is a pitfall at a certain stage of development, a morass into which the majority sink. You see, once magnetized with the higher consciousness, the easiest way is to go on seeking that continuously. Nevertheless, if there is to be further progress, the *movement* must be completed with each renewal of attainment.

Betty: I think I understand now. If I just stayed in my own magnetic harmony, my cyclical movement would be obstructed. But when I bring the higher force to someone else, then I have utilized for practical purposes what has flowed into me, and the principle of movement is established.

Invisible: This concept of movement is difficult to convey, because its nearest mental counterpart is of movement from one place to another, whereas what we are discussing is nearer to radiation. It is a sensation of action with a certain repose—a difficult thing to express. The life moving through you functions and goes forth, but not necessarily from one place to another or moving you along.

This sounds obscure, but it is really very simple. All there is to it is the acknowledgment of a sensation of spiritual alignment with what is above and what is below, permitting the force of the higher consciousness to flow through. That is the whole of these teachings. It seems so obvious and simple that sometimes it is hard for us to realize its difficulties. Yet it is truly amazing in its inclusive power, its extension of your own personality into that of others, where before you were content within yourself.

Betty: I see myself as I used to be, convinced of the essential tuning process, without which we are nothing; doing it more or less regularly; luxuriating in it, even. But now that picture is repellent to me: it has no joyous dynamics. The prospect ahead is ever so much more satisfactory. Where before the picture was like a lake, now it is a flowing river. It would be impossible after this for me to return to the apathetic stage— except periodically for rest, or if I became conscious of nervous tensions, or for healing if ill. Now that I feel the stupendous stir of making a current by opening my outlets, no longer could I *abide* the self-containment of the still-pond-no-more-moving days!

Invisible: It is the greatest of all sensations, this alignment with what might be called the Great Doing—this alignment of oneself with it, not merely to *feel*, passively, the flow, but to try out one's allotment of it, actively and enthusiastically.

In fact, what *is* enthusiasm but this? What is energy but this? What is love itself but this?—this removal of barriers, enabling force to flow forward or back as necessity dictates: forward to accomplishment of law forms in matter; backward to recharge and refresh in the primal force.

Betty: Even in my utmost moments of height and expansion I never realized what a limitless participation you could attain by aligning yourself this way. It is the most beautiful feeling imaginable: like being imbedded in an infinite life of warm, pulsating, desirable human qualities, immeasurably greater and more powerful than your own. That is the nearest I can come to describing it. If you can hold onto it, you can work down

185

through its lower manifestations and all the dragging, ignorant resistances to it, and remain quite undamaged by them because you are not vibrating to that level. But if you let go hands on either side of you, you break the greater current and contain only your little waning bit, for your allotment of power is absolutely dependent on your integrity of alignment. Unless you join hands in that way, you will not be entrusted.

There is a technique to this inflow-outflow business. But before going on to what was told us as to that, perhaps it may be as well to take time for one of Betty's more mystic experiences. To us it supplied a kind of larger atmosphere in which to suspend the more definite conceptions already given.

Betty: (After a long pause.) I found myself with a vast outlook over manifold life. It was so endlessly extensive compared to the narrow outlook I was accustomed to, I lost myself in it. Dazed and benumbed in all my sense, I struggled to perceive it all. It was so difficult that the old habit of contraction took possession of me. I said: I can't go any farther than this; I'll just gather this much in. So I started to work on collecting just the foreground of things to tell you about, and I got my circle drawn harder and tighter. I was so busy collecting that I lost all things beyond that foreground: I just reduced it to that and nothing else by trying to gather it in and possess it.

That was a *small* idea. I stopped to consider a moment and found I'd spoiled everything. I remembered how it had seemed in the beginning: the vast panorama of life and all the varied experiences coming as if broadcast to me. I had spoiled it all by trying to possess them after the manner of man.

Then something urged me to a different manner of

taking. I looked again and discovered a secret. I found I could broadcast *myself* to complete participation—which is true possession....

It is hard to tell you of this, because I know so little about it, but it rests on firm sane laws. It is hidden under the surface glint of materially desirable things. Those who never possess these sometimes find the secret of possession of all life; and those who have satiated themselves come painfully to starvation on golden platters: and some in between acquire the balance which directs them to the secret of possession.

I cannot grow in a moment to where I can describe this vivid contrast in the methods of ownership: ownership after the manner of man, and ownership by way of the law. I can only just sense it by looking at my associates here. Because today I am in the company of those who have completely abandoned self for the heritage of participating in the whole. They are absolutely dispossessed of things. They've grown into enormous, almost unlimited power by the strength of their aims. I don't understand it. I only know their power is a kind of selfless power which makes their position unrelated to any of the products we call possessions.

(Long pause.)

I was experimentally broadcasting myself to participation in the great elements of life, and I said: Why do I not come to dissolution of my individuality this way? And then I dimly sensed the use of that other gathering in, collecting instinct in its unperverted state. I sensed its ability to concentrate power collected to be utilized for the intelligent purposes of co-operation. But I'm too feeble and stupid to tell you much that is useful....

Here are two great forces. I must leave them there.

Invisible: The acquisitional sense that is usually directed towards the gathering together of things, like everything else, can be transposed to intangible, but still more valuable purposes. This acquisitive action is one of man's most useful characteristics, but its nature is two-fold: we can acquire by drawing entirely to ourselves and retaining what we have selected; or we can acquire from the Unlimited Supply what is necessary for the completion of a *forthgoing plan*. This latter, higher form is not the usual concept of acquisitiveness. It resembles more the ambition of the artist seeking materials for his creative purposes.

At present, of course, earth is in its grossly acquisitive, destructive childhood. All its pressure is downward toward itself, as is its gravitation. Thus all its habitants are imbued with the same, as it were, negative force. Any individual who has strength enough to overcome within himself this dead weight, and to make the first effort toward becoming an *outgoing*, radioactive, positive expression of life, comes in contact with an entirely new field of existence. And if he can *maintain* his reversed current of force; then in exchange for his contribution to the whole positive field, that entire field is his to draw upon in proportion as he acquires the wisdom to manipulate it.

This reversed current of life begins deep within each human heart. First there are whirlpools of confusion and suffering; then the passivity of mere desire; followed by the gathering strength of the outgoing current. This outgoing current is the consciousness that life is more than self; it is voluntary fusion with the dimly sensed greater self of endlessly expanding possibilities.

(Pause.)

Betty: Supposing you offered yourself completely and eagerly, joyously spent yourself on something because you wanted to more than anything else in the whole wide world; and while doing it you suddenly found you were receiving something beyond anything you had ever experienced before, so that you didn't know whether you were giving or taking; that would be the beautiful state, the beautiful union, this wonderful thing we are trying to get hold of and are evolving toward. That, in its highest form, is equilibrium.

Think how we use flour and various other things, all perfectly good in themselves, but valueless until put together in process to make bread. It is just so with our "duties" and various conscientious efforts: they are not much good unless they are blended and put through processes connected with desire, lightheartedness, affection, eagerness—all the good mixers.

The word "will-power" is not appropriate here. Willpower is a tearing loose of fruit, instead of waiting for it to ripen. The other way, of counting on your supreme power, is the ripened way. It works strongly and harmoniously, without jar and nerve wreckage.

CHAPTER II

NATURAL RESOURCES

The conception of the higher consciousness as something that flowed through was illuminating. But it was a trifle vague. It needed definition. What was it that flowed? How did it feel? What did one *do* about it? And, above all, what should one *not* do about it? We recoiled, instinctively, against any smug idea of going forth to dispense Sweetness and Light.

The Invisibles must have sensed these reactions in us, for next they took up our materials for action, what might be called the natural resources of the higher consciousness. As usual, they began through one of Betty's symbolic experiences.

Betty: (After a long pause.) Each time I do this particular adjustment I am experimentally dead. It is a very delicate adjustment. I recognize it by the fact that I am absolutely reduced to a dot of consciousness in cosmos. Everything accustomed of habits and surroundings and outside considerations has dropped

190

away. I am alone with my residue....

But there is a difference from last time. I used to start right in wanting to absorb something, to feed, to grasp, to sort of suck in something. I was dependent on what I was capable of reaching out and getting and digesting. Now it is different. Now I actually have a little something of my own to give. I am still absorbing, still feeding, but it is not my exclusive occupation any more. In addition I have a bit of self-controlled power, and I'm trying to find a way to use it.... (Pause.)

I don't know what's being done. Looks like a photograph being taken. I've just got to stay still and be content while it's being done....

(Long pause with many ejaculations of surprise.)

That was a very, very memorable experience! I think I'll tell you about it first, and then they'll amplify it more intelligently. You may not get the point of it at first, but it is an important symbol.

A perfect surface was prepared—a perfectly new vital surface. I helped by recollecting untracked snow, ocean-swept sand, and the sprays of waterfalls—all the most vital beauty-blending things I have experienced. I just lay quiet and did it until I realized I had helped to create a perfect, unused, impressionable surface. Then they whispered it was for the impress of my heart. I didn't know what that meant, but very gently they explained that my spirit must rest on the surface, naturally and quietly, to make a picture of myself for me, a mold of myself with characteristic outlines, like a clever, vivid sketch, a few salient features unamplified.

I rested as they told me, in a passive sort of way, until it was borne in on me that unconsciously I was doing something more. It was not that I was giving myself out in such a way as to make any strong impress on the plastic surface. At first it seemed more like just containing myself dynamically, but without vigorous contact with it. Then suddenly a force radiated from within me, and around me an impress quickly deepened. I felt it taking shape like a satisfying mold of a beautiful vase, or something that can be used for others' enjoyment. They say this is a very important symbol, introducing a new step in our progress.

Invisible: If the development already accomplished is to be utilized, by whatever means we can devise we must strive to give you a certain concept. Unfortunately there exists no available avenue of approach to it. Grooves must be made, avenues prepared for the intellectual acceptance. Therefore we begin with this seemingly child's play imagery, in order to give an inkling of the reality which will afterward find expression in verbally handleable concept.

Now the point is this: there exists in you, indefinitely developable, an engine of power, dynamically creative, capable of impressing and molding your material world according as you give out from your inner being its creative force. This force is not primarily the *mentally* creative force, which you understand perfectly. It is the higher sense of that mentally creative force, the vital principle of life; and comes, not from that mere agent of the soul, the intellect, but from the very plexus of life itself. The mental force can make a mold or plan, but for completion this plan must have its vital principle supplied. It is the neatly made electric globe into which the current is not turned. The true creative force, on the other hand, carries its own vital principle with it. It is a matter of the heart as well as the clearly seen concept of the mind.

(Pause; Betty chuckled.)

Betty: I started laughing because it seemed so absurd to me to call this vast indulgence of happiness such dreary words as "the life principle." I said to myself: no wonder nobody gets excited about a thing called "the life principle"! And I laughed at the comparison of that with the thing, the radiating thing itself.

This helped a lot: it gave at least an impression of the central factor, and outlined in a general way the field of action. But detail still lacked. It was like a moving picture out of focus: there was a vague impression of something doing, but nothing definitely recognizable.

Presently the Invisibles set about sharpening the focus.

Betty: (After a pause.) They are showing me the great secret of will-power. I can see it work over and over again. It's a process of making pleasurable your will-power. The minute you make it pleasurable, combining with the heart solvent, it starts working, like a chemical affinity, lending warmer vitality to your object, making it work itself naturally....

I don't see much of this strain and duty and uninspired effort around, this heaviness of work which all of us go through to accomplish things. We weren't meant to work with heaviness; it's a discordant condition. Work should be just fun. What a pity that the tradition of work has become so painful!

Invisible: We want to substitute in your minds for the stiff words "will-power" the same idea in terms of natural exuberance. You think highly of will-power because it accomplishes certain obvious results of self-propulsion. But look how hard you run in tennis, or walk in fishing or doing something you like. That is another sort of self-propulsion; easier, because you are in harmony with what you are doing. That harmony isn't generally recognized as part of the lifting force; yet it is so much more effective a way than this painful will-power business. One is done with your united being; and the other in spite of your divided being.

(Pause.)

Betty: I feel so loose-jointed and full of play! As though I were tiptoeing up to a joke on somebody, with all the jolly and exquisite painstaking you can so readily and easily put into a joke. In an instant I'll shout and laugh with the sheer gleeful exhilaration of it!

Invisible: Such occasions are natural whole moments of ideal combination that you inadvertently hit upon. Anything would be possible to you in these moments. It doesn't matter what your object may be, playing games or the business of life, this combination is the secret of man's fullest possibility.

(Pause.)

Betty: There's something about a force which this feeling is akin to, or related to....I'll have to go deeper to get it....

(Long Pause.)

I'm trying to get a clear idea of this spreading, creative, radiant thing I'm associating with. It is a supporting force pertaining to the reach just above us. I'd like to get in it and be swept along with it, but I don't think I'm ready. It goes on to such a vast ocean beyond my comprehension....

It's so nameless I don't know where to begin to cut it up into words. If I do that, I'm afraid it won't piece together again. It's too big for language. All I can say is that it's the biggest union of life, the nearest harmony, the most collected force....

Harmony is so poor a word! It isn't a *bad* word; it's just a mistreated word. I want to get that *fresh*. Now it's just a semi-religious, semi-musical term; but there is a rising tide of progress connected with it. In spite of its inadequacy it represents a strong factor in this force that upholds, this tide of extension. But it is not the thing itself—only a shred....

It's not will-power, either; that's only another aspect

194

of it; just one more place where we've touched it in comprehension. What I am trying to get at is the whole of this force; not only the detached bits we recognize in words of will-power and concentration, but the complete force of it. Don't you see? Will-power and concentration are just a spear of the mind, penetrating. Unless the bulk of you is inspired with some larger capacity for following up and attaining what the mind thrusts at, the spear alone is useless.

Invisible: Concentration is a word appropriate to the mind. Discard it. Get the fuller idea of it in the sense of naturally, and easily, without tension, gathering and holding yourself in harmony with the strength of the higher consciousness. There is a great difference between this and the nervous restricted force of mental concentration on a thing you seek with your own strength alone. Get the two ideas: keep them apart. Holding yourself in harmony is what lets in the higher power, makes the process a natural one, without strain. The other idea, of concentration, shuts out all but what you have in mind.

Concentration is a dangerous word. So is will-power. Both of these are centered in the mind, whereas this greater power is definitely divorced from the mind. Mind is the planning organ; but that which carries out the plans is the real executive. This force is to will-power what will-power is to the mind.

Betty: I don't know yet what that real executive of you is called. I can only sense it without being able to bring it back: an upholding, progressing force occupying the complete circuit of my vision. It expands so far beyond, that I have lost even the speck I called will-power. What *is* this big thing? If I only had another steppingstone to it besides will-power, another known symbol! That one doesn't go any distance: I can't get there with it.

Invisible: There is always a contracted and an expanded form of everything. Will-power is the contracted form of this higher thing. You can step into it from will-power without contracting if you think of it more as *desire power*. Will-power is in spite of your desires; doubling the pressure.

(Pause.)

Betty: I'm still tormented by the lack of a symbol for that spreading, living, capturing force....

It is like trying to look at the stars in the daytime: it's perfectly clear until I bring it into the daylight of words, and then it's gone!

The Invisibles hammered away at this idea over a period of months, adding a hint here and a suggestion there, with an occasionl full-length discourse thrown in. Space does not permit complete quotation, but the following will help to round out:

Invisible: (After a long pause, occupied in the study of something "wordless" and much groping for a name.) Intense reciprocity.

Betty: That won't do. Reciprocity is national; this is something warm and near and embraceable. A great heart hunger for it is possessing me.

Invisible: It's the great and simple secret of further progress, and true possession of what has been developed.

Betty: It would take a poet or an angel to express it, because we do not know how to partake of this superhappiness. I get just a breath of it when I lie down next the earth and sniff it; and I get just a taste of it when I come in on the waves and the salt is on my lips; and I get just a whisper of it when I stay still in the woods and listen; and I get the most of it when I love something, even my dog or my garden. Don't you see; I want so much to sink deep, dive, be absorbed in this intense reciprocity, this thing I can't even name. It must be experienced and entered completely in order to have practical understanding and sympathy and accomplishment in the material world. It gives an endless vista....

I don't think I can say this: I'll try.

As soon as I arrive at this superhappiness, this suspension, this equilibrium of health and happiness, it must return me to acute perception of the lack of it in the world. It rushes from its force into weakness, like the great physical law of the vacuum; it rushes to it. That explains the eagerness to help us of those who have acquired it over here. It is the basis of all true service....

There's a lot more I don't get hold of. It touches that beautiful, almost perfect word, sympathy. How did that word get spoiled? *Constructive* sympathy: that is the pinnacle of human experience. It is not sorrowing with people; it is sharing the inspiration overflowing from your abundance. This abundance will not exist if you allow the restrictions of the lower dimension of sympathy.

Stewart: What do you mean by lower dimension of sympathy?

Betty: Mere stagnant, unvitalized pity, unrelated to the source of inspiration. That is the way I've always felt: I've always been *sufferingly* sympathetic; and now, momentarily, I feel *constructively* sympathetic. At times, in the pain of discords, I've ached with acute perception of the wrongness of things. But if I could keep this greater power I could go beyond that: I could help heal things. It can't be done with any success, however, unless this percolation of superior force takes place. Slowly it must be acquired. The well-being and happiness are the dominant thing about it, and the over-flow is a natural consequence.

197

Do you not see that this stage of instruction is but the putting of flesh on the skeleton of your "records"? If you stop where they are, you have no more than a plan for action. This clothing with the warm flesh of the living emotional life is what will bring you the meaning of all past efforts, the goal of everything hitherto attempted. It is the hardest of all to convey, because the recording of it but transposes it back to the skeleton plan. Nevertheless, if you are to complete the cycle of your previous intake of inspiration, your heart must now have its time of emotional output.

Your present task is no longer a reaching up for more. It is utilization of what you have, propelled by yourself; not tensely in the mind-driven way, but intensely in the ardor of the heart.

CHAPTER III

DISTRIBUTION

Normally, our first obligation in life, anywhere, is to keep a whole skin. In a new country, especially, we must watch our step. It is sure to be full of pitfalls and dangers. Sometimes keeping our own skin whole is a full-time job. But, sooner or later, we must find that it cannot continue to be the only consideration. Other people enter the picture. From then on our responsibility is increased many fold.

In dealing with the higher consciousness this time comes when we feel the urge to pass it on to others. We have discovered what to us is new country; we have gained possession of something fresh and exciting. We are convinced of its value. We are wildly enthusiastic about it. Our natural impulse, then, is to share it with our friends. It is more than an impulse, more than a desire. It is an obligation, a serious obligation, a solemn duty to Do Good in the World. Let's set about it! At once!

That is a danger spot. That is how bores and nuisances, zealots, fanatical reformers come into being. Those are not pleasant or welcome persons. Even when they are right, they are wrong; for their very over-enthusiastic persistence fills the average man with a perverse desire to go the other way. I suppose this is one of the most perilous spots of country one has to cross in his excursion toward the unknown.

Yet it is, after all, merely a matter of the technique of distribution: and on that technique our Invisibles next centered their instruction. The familiar symbolic approach:

Betty: I am back in that wide vaulted life of boundless possibilities, but I can't for the life of me act in it. There seems to be something checking me—some problem I must solve. You see, I've completed the stage of conception and am approaching the stage of production....

(Pause.)

It's as if the sun were shining, but illuminated just the tops of the trees, the upper layers of the world, leaving in shadow the lower affairs of life. The big response in me is all to the beauty which the sun is revealing by its reflection. The vaulted life is like that. But the things in the shadow that aren't reflecting the sun are what I must reach and work among.

(Long pause.)

I wish I could tell you about that. I stepped out of the sun into the shadow, bringing with me all the memory of its warmth and fullness of life. Before the radiation of it leaves me, I've got to use it. Down in the chilling shadows of the world I am entrusted with this vision of the warmth and fullness of life as an illuminating and quickening power. It warms and lights your life as electricity does houses; and it is just as real and just as possible. It should be named—like electricity. Then people would acknowledge it, seek it, acquire it. To make it available, all it needs is to be taken out of the old distant celestial covering it has been wrapped in.

(Pause.)

You know those games they play with a ball, in which you are not allowed to use your hands? That's something the way it is with me now. It's as though authority had been given me to go ahead and accomplish, but I don't know how to go about it. I must puzzle it out....

It's a great problem: I have gradually to grow around it. At present I can only be sure that I feel two things. One is a kind of basic relationship—a kind of static power of harmonious adjustment. That's mine to take and to develop indefinitely. But it's not *doing* anything....

The other thing is the release of that established force. Just how this is done I don't understand at all. I am only sure that this basic static strength can be sent out in an assimilable form, and taken up by almost anybody. Sometimes it seems to just *feel* its way out—just seep out like water, feeling its way through every available channel.

I'm afraid I haven't accomplished much today, but I have felt as though deprived of all my sense perceptions. It has been as if my hands and feet and eyes were bound, and I was told to go ahead and experiment. Naturally I have been pretty much at a loss.

But I did do *something*. Do you want to know what I did? It is sort of a foolish thing to tell; but the first thing I did was to throw out all the warmth and happiness I could collect and hurl forth. I decided I was at least going to have my own circumambience that everybody would like to come into!

As it turned out, this effort of Betty's which she thought so foolish, proved to be the key to the whole situation. Her further experience and instruction soon made this evident.

Betty: (After a long pause.) They are all around me and could help me, but they want me to dig it out for myself. You get much farther along when you dig it out for yourself. That is the reason they sometimes just throw me overboard this way.

(Pause.)

I'm working at the idea of releasing the permeation. I *consciously outgo*. It's like tide pressure. I'm unbarriered toward human beings. It's not that I'm artificially capturing them in a socially "charming" sense: that's such an imitation thing. The real thing works of itself, after you have established control over your barriers. It's a pity to dissect it. It is natural and simple between friends, but we use it too preciously when we might squander it.

Invisible: Alongside of spiritual consciousness must be established propulsion of the vitality you accumulate. This you do not at present accomplish, in the sense of habitual output. We must clear up your understanding of this before we can go further.

In the first place, it is fundamentally an emotion or feeling, a sensation of throwing out from you—not an *idea to be expressed*. You do not work with material implements, such as words: you work by having plenty of this superior force to give. It is an active, superabundant sort of sympathy that naturally overflows and helps to do for others what has already been done for you. It is like a magnet or a chemical attraction that draws out of them a similar quality, and gets them started with their own effort....

Betty: It sounds silly, but it seems strangely like a heart fluid. We don't recognize a heart fluid, do we?

201

Invisible: Heart is the nearest word you have. It contains the most ingredients of this new force.

When you want to be of help to people, always remember that what you must work with is not a brain impulse, but a heart impulse. Don't struggle with people in the tight little bottled-up medium of the intellect—don't be a Miss Fixit. Just flood them quietly, silently, persistently with this heart fluid. They won't know it, won't see it, but they'll soak it up a little when they are off guard. This is the first principle of dealing with people.

Betty: It's like old magic. I never did see anything so silent as that pussyfooting force. Delicious: so quiet and so sure and so enfolding—so beautifully enfolding and permeating!

Invisible: Strangely enough, this force is the same as the curative power so many people are beginning to recognize—both self-curative and administrative. Margaret* doesn't understand altogether how or why she gets hers. She gets it because she puts her hands on either side a person with confidence and outfling of desire to help; and just to the extent she does this naturally and vigorously the force flows in. It is the *same force*, only modified to harmonize and act directly on the body.

Betty: If you keep in touch with it, you can always exchange strength with people, even when they are going down for the third time—or when you are. I've often been replenished by people just when my courage was lowest—and they didn't preach at me, either. They just looked as though they were walking in the happiest way.

---

* Margaret Cameron, who discovered, quite empirically, that by placing her hands either side a sufferer, she seemed to induce a healing "current" between them.

Invisible: It is most important not to think of this as a pious, posey, parsony sort of thing. There is nothing at all of the See-how-holy-and-calm-I-am idea about it. Nor is it any affectation of a benign pussy-cat smile toward all humanity. Nearer to the genuine thing would be the beautiful word sincerity. Nobody has ever tarnished that word, because so few use it completely. It is being yourself, your best inner self, so naturally and freely that you contribute from it to the inner selves of others. That is offering something simple and sound and true, instead of irritating people with benign shallowness.

The safest way is *not to bother about working it in detail at all.* The minute you begin to figure consciously how it is going to work, you are in danger of becoming pious. If you leave it alone it will work itself, without pose or effort, automatically—like heat drying up dampness, or a sun ray expanding a thing. You see, in reality it is never a question of painstakingly doing carefully considered acts. It is more a question of continuously giving back, continuously throwing off from you the surplus vitality of understanding, sympathetic perception. If this through process is acquired, it will keep open a channel through which inspiration will come for the necessary individual acts.

Putting these things into words makes them sound complicated and stiff-jointed and difficult, like the elaborate descriptions of process you read, which are so simple when someone actually shows you how. Too bad; but it can't be helped. Just remember that, however stilted and painful this thing may sound, as a matter of fact it is actually the most joyously free action, the most simple living you can imagine.

(Pause.)

Betty: There's such a vast difference between the philanthropic idea of doing good deeds and feeling gen-

erous about it, and this eager, avid-for-health work—
this pumping of new life into things because you have
so much of it, and want to extend farther and farther the
living, loving, laughing area. By comparison the conventional idea of "service" is such a pale, insignificant
shadow....

A tree is almost a perfect symbol of the real thing:
earth-nourished at its base, sun-worshipping in its top,
spreading to include all it can in its great amplitude.
Unconsciously it gives back to earth after its own
fashion. It doesn't have to trouble itself with "good
deeds"!

As often happened, shortly after this analysis, the
idea was synthesized for Betty by an intense and com-
prehensive experience of the thing itself.

Betty: (After a long pause.) I am doing such curious
exercises: I'll tell you about them later....

You remember that business of intensifying your
out-going impulses? Well, the exercise I've been doing
is like that, only it is no longer in a straight-line
channel, as it were. I am getting the circular radiation
of it, like a lawn sprinkler. I keep turning it, almost like
a searchlight: the beam is like a searchlight ray, only
it's all warm and human and happy and natural enthusiasm and interest, as when one approaches one's
hobbies, affections or loves. I am exercising myself by
turning a complete circle with it. At each point it
touches I see with new and sympathetic eyes right into
the soul of the thing, and my kinship and responsibil-
ities with it....

I don't actually have to turn myself now; I can do it in
almost any direction....

Now they've taken it away. It was to give greater
flexibility to the idea of propulsion....*Radiation* is

better. That was an actual practice in radiation....

There's something more about it; but I've got to go deeper to get it....

(Pause.)

I am getting strength almost beyond my ability to contain....I lead a dance, I fling, I spread warmth, I rush on, incandescent with life! Just let me travel on in this glowing way for a while....

(Long pause.)

I am going through a change, a curious radiating, convexing and pouring out from myself, as definite as though I'd been turned inside out....

Why! When you're arranged in that concave shape, you present no surface of participation in life! You are an alien shape, just a dormant seed-encasement of life! I don't want to be that way again, ever, just concavely containing my little bit. It is all right, but it is ungerminated.

(Long pause.)

Take something exhilarating: deep blue sky and yellow leaves, the poised stillness of the last days of life— take a salt-sea-washed body and the cool sweet union of it with the great fresh element. Keep going out, out, out beyond the mere exhilaration of these. You have turned the other way, curving out, a radiation of yourself—radiation....

I don't quite understand that: too big for me. I have the feeling of it: I know what it feels like to manifest in various forms of life. But I can work only in the emotional desire of it: I can't tell what my words are doing. I can only radiate myself: it's my only form of expression....

I wish I could stir you up to experience this one glorious moment. It is as though I were standing by you asleep. I'll be asleep myself soon....

Now I've got to refocus, diminish my vision, come

205

back to a little optical thing. It is a curious sensation to come back! As I drift down, the main impression I keep is that nothing is so far-reaching as this radiation—nothing! Sending out books and talks and experiments and everything else is limited, compared to the radius of this personal influence. The living exponent convinces; books can reflect, but not convince. Books....I don't know how to say that, but it's embalming ideas. Don't you see? Embalming them in books and records....

(Pause; laughed.)

I was thinking of the difference, as regards their effect on us, between museums filled with the reconstructed skeletons of things, and the live animals themselves walking around. That is why philosophies get nowhere: they are like an empty shell something once was in.

In the weeks that followed, the Invisibles, over and over again, urged upon Betty the practice of this new phase, and as time passed, her understanding of it widened. The following is one of her later, more complete statements of the process:

Betty: I am getting a glimpse of the harmonizing power of this force in its essence, and it is so tremendous that I don't *dare* try to tell you. It puts such a new interpretation on everything. It *is* creative force: it *is* the essence of life of all things—and you can't handle the essence of life with your finite mind! I am overawed and dumbfounded by it. It is like some supreme stimulation of each thing up to the limits of its perfection within its laws. It is an ordering magic. Its most diluted form—which is the only form I am capable of daring to handle—applied to a jumble of disarranged, ill-functioning, perverted life of any kind, passing over

206

it, magically orders it. I see the little laws all working busily, righting themselves. It functions beautifully and naturally now; and before, it was so jumbled....

But I'd better not try to tell you about it—I couldn't. (Pause; then reluctantly.)

I suppose I really ought to tell you *something* of how I use it—only I don't know how to start....

Invisible: Begin by supposing you were trying to make your way in an ordinary day of ordinary activities. You would feel more or less like a trickling stream finding a way among leaves and twigs of the forest floor. That would be the lesser way of working, giving way to obstacles and being deflected by all the greater and more established bodies in your way.

Betty: I am saying to myself: that's the way the stream of my life *would* have worked. But how about it now, with this new power?

I don't shoot straight ahead with a superior overriding force. I hardly even plan. I seem at first just to stand tip-toe and look ahead at my objective, as it were. Then I busy myself generating a great and composed secure determination, quite different from nervous willpower. It is a great confident recognition of my ability to get there. Only I seem to work very hard at the generating; as if I actually produced warmth, or as if I actually made light, where it was dark, in order to see the way. I can't seem to say anything that fits, because conditions vary according to what I would accomplish, but fundamentally it is always a generating of harmony.

Invisible: Let us expand this idea of inner generation. We have taken it away from the brain, because it must have warmth and emotional content, and have made it a new region, nearer to heart indulgence. This inner generation steps up human life as definitely as electrical potentials are increased. And in the beginning, strangely enough, the keeping it alive and glowing

207

within one is a larger part of one's personal contribution than the definite utilization of it for any detailed purpose. If it exists, it has its own aura, its light and heat aura, its zone of action; and those around you can start induction from it—generally without being aware of it. Because you do not understand its laws of dissemination, you are inclined to deprecate its apparent inactivity as selfish indulgence. On the contrary, it must be accepted on its own terms. It radiates best when you do not interfere with it.

Betty: There are a great many working in exactly this way now—in the discarnate. You have no idea how amusing it is, while you are still in a physical body, to be associating with a discarnate method of work!

(Chuckled.)

I feel like a smudge pot keeping off the frost. That's all I can do now....Well, it's something! It helps the climate—temporarily.

Invisible: Now everything is twofold. To this must be added another aspect more nearly akin to the human brain and will-power. That is the refinement of use following after, when the inner generation becomes established. Always must be kept the primary state as an active association; but from this, in due and proper sequence, you proceed to bring to focus through the projector of your own individual power.

Betty: Now I am coming to the next step: I actually throw out from my confidence and clarity of aim everything that I have in me of warming and magnetizing progressive life power—I actually work at producing that around myself, until the flow of it reaches further and further. It is like a blanketing of my entire problem with this harmonizing determination which I somehow spin out of my being.

Invisible: Everybody can do at least this, even though blind to the process: that is, contribute the greatest outpouring each is capable of manufacturing. However ill-fitted his education or abilities of any kind, each is capable of exercising this quality. Confronted with a problem, he at once plugs in, as it were—becomes an outlet or a conduit or a channel. Of course it takes practice for some types of mind to get automatic action in this incubating, blanketing, brooding vitalization of things. But in time anyone can progress to the point where it glows over him at odd moments with reminders to work some more that way.

Betty: I cannot think anywhere in my experience of any belief or religion which has taught quite this. Of course the acts manifesting your beliefs are the ordinary mechanism of progress, but this what I call blanketing business is a tremendously advanced process of preparation *for* the acts manifesting your beliefs. It is the harmonious way to go about them. We cannot always succeed in our act—we are thwarted by others and handicapped by our meager abilities—but in the generating of creative harmony there are no limits to anyone's possibilities.

Invisible: All this clumsy effort to put down what may seem obvious or ineffectual or vaporish according to one's temperament—if you could see more of it, you would realize that it is a first step, and the nearest we can come to directing your feet on the path towards the highest creative force. A developed person, even a developing one, who has come into some recognition of this power expanding within him, has the opportunity of utilizing it over the most commonplace episodes of daily life. It works very much like water let loose on parched ground. Not too great a volume of water at first; but the life-giving spirit of it creeping and seeping, everywhere supplying the quickening element that releases the fertility stored in the dusty brown earth. It is just this gentle distribution around you of the spiritual heart force, as you feel its expansion within you, that will teach you the actuality of spiritual faculties. It is not a directed irrigation like so-called mental treatment; it is more the rising stream finding its level in the open places among natural encouragements and resistances.

This is the natural, most successful method of giving spiritual first aid. Lay out, or let spread out, across the level of your life your own steadily maintained spiritual convictions, perhaps unexpressed, but none the less radiating. You will not know when you help: it will not matter! The important thing is to recognize and utilize this great unseen power: to make your life function in this outgoing fashion until it is no longer possible for you to contract against the informing impulses of the higher consciousness.

At first your little stream will doubtless find its way only in diffused efforts hither and thither, seeking a path in which to flow. But just as water tends to unify itself in a bed where there is least resistance, so you too must feel your way to pouring your vivified consciousness across your environment. Do this eagerly and persistently enough over a long enough period of time, and you will achieve that highest of all desirables, the creation of a channel of steady spiritual flow.

To conclude this subject of distribution I offer the following, without comment except to underscore that of the Invisibles themselves: it certainly *is* lofty teaching! But if you don't peer too closely, this kind of a high lookout sometimes affords the most inclusive view of all.

Betty: This is one of the most expanding days I've had. It is as if a great magnet drew me by force of kinship, by overwhelming warmth extracted me from my individual self to conscious, joyous participation in the universal life....

I have temporarily grown into the possession of a vast sympathetic nervous system or heart awareness. The pulse of the world pulses through me. The breath of common life is in my lungs. All human emotions ripple over me as impartially as a breeze over the ocean. This is a tremendous experience. How am I to face separation again?....

The message is embodied at this point. I must get it.

Invisible: This is very advanced teaching. We are not sure that it is wise to precipitate it, but will sketch its meaning. Very briefly and crudely, it is to this effect:

The undeveloped being lives in isolation of consciousness within himself, his village, his town, his country, depending on how far along he is, always contained within definite personality limits, separated from other creations by the confines of his senses and sympathies. The developed man is as different a creature in the breadth of his perceptions as a walnut differs from the winds. The developed man can search out any distance with an extension of himself, his full consciousness concentrated at any point he desires. He assumes kinship with other consciousnesses as poignantly as with his own.

Betty: It is just like the radio: you pick out the right wave length and travel on it.

Invisible: This sympathic assumption of kinship empowers him with the attributes of the higher consciousness. And one result of this is that he is no longer, while living as other men, restricted by their limitations of position—position in the geometrical sense—because anything he turns his attention to ardently, anything he loves, he *becomes* in this greater entity. It gives him the ability to broadcast himself, to travel to it sympathetically, as it were, on its individual wave length.

211

Betty: It may not sound like much at first, but think of the stupendous power of this faculty when one actually grows into full possession of it. One no longer occupies a one-pointed position. One's heart extensions are potentially universal....

What are the attributes of this greater, this potentially universal, entity—this aggrandizement of consciousness? What, I ask myself, am I to do with it now that I am in it—how am I to utilize it? While here I can reach out and quicken the thoughts and heart of any human being I have ever known. What then? What right have I? How do I dare utilize that power, and for what purpose? I cannot see the answers to these questions now. I only know that one who has experienced this power, even momentarily, can never again be satisfied as the walnut in its shell.

Western civilization must purify Eastern mysticism of its dormant quality by evolving energized occultism. It must grasp with strong practical hands the principles which mostly have only floated through men's brains. The genius of vitality must be applied to this superlife which has been but a dream of detached occultists, modifying it, energizing the ideal of spiritual life; but modifying also your materialism. The occultism known as superpower wanes in Eastern civilization through fatalistic inertia. Superimposed on Western energy it will make great strides in raising the level of average human possibilities of attainment.

It needs the affectional or enthusiastic element to enable the force of the higher consciousness to carry out far, instead of being all diffused near at hand. That requires something definite outside the first inner and personal preoccupations with oneself. Even a dog or a sunset or a bird is a good start. But the first stirring of creative power comes most easily in outgoing to a fellow-sufferer, in rapport and sympathy of understanding of another's trouble. It is the line of least resistance for the divine spark to seek in arousing itself.

CHAPTER IV

FABRICATION

The foregoing, I realize, is pretty hard sledding. Nevertheless, any effort of understanding will be more than repaid, for there is where we touch the farthest north of these teachings. This "inner generation" approach to our problems is the secret of living. Could we accomplish that fully we would come into possession of a device that would bring to us, almost automatically, every other desirable. And by no means abstract or theoretical desirables only; but, in one way or another, everything the most practical hardhead could demand.

Fantastic? Not at all. But neither is it as easy as the sit-down-and-manifest school of thought would have us believe. To accomplish it we must apprehend it: and to apprehend a thing we must experience it—which takes time and patience. But it works. I can testify to that.

At this point there is a likely looking branch trail, the more plausible because, apparently, it is headed for high ground. A good many people, as soon as they begin to get aspirations and a little "occult knowledge," go astray on it, not as multitudinously, perhaps, as those who go shouting off on the proselytizing-missionary dead-end, but even more obstinately. It is an attractive trail, for it combines a pleasing sense of holiness with a nice easy grade.

According to its travel-agents the best way to alleviate the sufferings of humanity is to retire permanently into the solitudes, mentally or physically, of the Higher Life. From this vantage point one is to broadcast beatific vibrations into the turmoil of humanity.

This idea gains enormous prestige on the authority of somewhat fragmentary reports concerning the "Masters" of Eastern occultism. And there is considerable weight of evidence to back it. But—and this is the crucial point, and is also self-evident—in order to do it successfully one must be a "Master"!

To reverse this reasoning is dangerous—and cock-eyed as well. It parallels the classic syllogism; a horse has four legs; this beast has four legs; therefore this beast is a horse. A "Master" works best as a hermit; therefore if we work as hermits, we become "masters." Where is the difference?

From the very beginning the Invisibles prepared us against this fallacy. Not, at first, directly, but in

214

hints—a sentence here, a paragraph there—urging our hearty participation in everyday life, discountenancing any tendency toward withdrawal. Finally, to make sure we did not misinterpret and retire into solitary "radiation," they delivered a frontal attack.

Betty: (After a pause.) There seems to be only half a structure, and I don't know why....

They say the reason the other half is empty is because I've been on the way up. It won't be filled until I come down. They are showing me this as a warning not to dilute myself, not to scatter myself too much....

(Pause.)

I see it perfectly now: of course I couldn't go on being spun out of that psychic substance without a fixative of some kind. I have the spiritual reality, but now I must search among the things of the world which we already possess, in order to assemble some material image of my convictions. They must no longer remain general and vague: they must be specialized, to focus, to make points of contact. Even the littlest specializations count—the simplest, most trivial incidents to triumph over. It is like cutting little funny places for your toes to get in when you climb....

It is an enormous task, this business of substantiation, and I have very little idea of the shaping process. But I do realize the absolute necessity for me to embody. I feel it more than I can say: I feel the balance and the need of it. Unless I do it, I'll just wander off and get thinner and thinner....

Your part seems so different. You don't take as much intuitively, but you substantiate better. It's the opposite from me: I take more than I am capable of managing, and it is waste. It is not properly assimilated and converted to something useful for others.

That is what I must remedy.

Invisible: A person susceptible to the simple purity of the higher consciousness is apt to be contented with what is in reality only the seed, and have little imagination as to the flower. As a matter of fact these first stages, held apart from life and labeled spirituality, have actually a sterile quality. At this point in the individual's development, in order to attain a closer integration with the higher consciousness, much is stripped away of sense perceptions. In consequence there is an unavoidable loss of the form of the thing, and if the aspirant stops there, very little of usable product can result. It is much as if the seed of a plant were shipped from the place in which it is indigenous, to a far country; and as if, in that far country, the recipient were content to possess the seed, and did not plant it.

No seed is of any use unless you establish its cultural necessities. You feel instinctively, even in the figurative case of those people who possess a spiritual seed which they merely guard with faith, but with bafflement. And you feel it likewise in offering instinctive homage to the full flower of any plant, be it of the lowliest and earthiest. Consequently, although the seed of the higher consciousness has been given you, you must acknowledge there remains the necessity of planting it. We are about to proceed, therefore, with the cultural directions, more eager than you for the flowering.

Betty: (Long pause.) I am working on my new problem, trying to see what it needs for solution....

Mostly I seem to want common ordinary earth brute force. Spirituality on earth is impotent without it: it is the functioning body of the spirit. They have concentrated me on the spiritual until I have gained a certain amount, and now I have to produce the force to make it function. If I just kept on with the spiritual, I'd get only a weak thing that would convince nobody.

Invisible: It is essential not to underrate the importance of physical vitality. It has a part in spiritual effort that isn't clearly recognized. The nearer the animal, the more the physical aggression, the more conspicuously effective is the individual in daily life. Philosophy and religion, on the other hand, tend in the opposite direction, diminishing the animal, and at the same time the force that functions in daily life. The vision that maintains its vigor is rare.

The chief trouble with the world today is that the limited, narrow ones are so noisy and active, while the wider broader ones are so silent and passive. The putting of your vitality into combination with your vision: that is the great necessity now. But do not mistake what that implies. The combined strength of vision and vitality is not aggressive and noisy and conspicuous. It is simply invincible, powerful, superior in the magic of its transmitting power, its magnetizing, vitalizing, quickening force.

Betty: That's it: spiritual vigor; it must get away from any idea of passivity. That is the whole trouble with these restrained, passively religious people. If they'd just stop thinking about restraining themselves on other things! There are no ironed-out, passive saints on the horizon of all; that's an entire misconception. Far better to burst bounds sometimes trying vigorously....

Invisible: It is this passive attitude which has made people think that using the higher consciousness is an impractical way of working at things. But it is impractical only when you merely conceive a noble idea and then sit back and expect some magic to accomplish it. The brute force man, in the meantime, goes out—perhaps with a lot of destructive function and antagonism

217

of unripened force—and tears things up, but accomplishes it somehow.

The combination of these two methods is what you want. The first step must always be a tremendous work of generating your harmony of conditions toward your ideal; *but* there is also the recognition of the practical method of accomplishing each step as it presents itself—the seizing of the opportunity. The best results are always a question of proportion between these two—a question of balancing the higher vision with the human fibre, so that you can actually *produce* your highest dreams and ideals, just as the practical man produces his limited ones. That would be the complete method of the *whole* man. This combination must be worked on a great deal if you are to produce the higher consciousness through an efficient machinery.

Betty: I wonder why they have to develop so many people in that lopsided way. They can't seem to make them whole. They have to specialize, and then put two or three together to accomplish one person's work. It's hard to understand this, but I see the problem it makes. There's the ideal on one side and the practical on the other, and the job is the almost impossible combination. That will be hard work, but it must be done to make the result a success. Dreamers stop short of that, whereas the practical man hurts his usefulness by cutting himself off from his source of inspiration.

Invisible: Usually one man dreams a dream, and another man takes it up; and the dreamer scorns his fixing of it as a low materialism. What these teachings are supposed to do is to open the gates of inspiration to the practical man, and to give creative construction power to the one who has vision but cannot share it by producing it. In the latter case the whole process is a development of fiber, tempering, stability and strength which, carried on, must *force* him to produce, to materialize—

218

or else make him acutely conscious that he is arresting his vision. For then he cannot help comprehending the true purpose of his visions, and realizing that they are not selfishly his to bury himself in, with scorn of the blind ones.

That is where all this is leading to, and that is the next point of attack: this adjustment of the ideal and the practical. In time it must bring about what is in reality the highest desirable of life. The race has always touched it in its great moments, but conscious understanding has lacked. That is the combination, the perfect blend, of spiritual inflow with earth embodiment and function.

Betty: It is going to be a great work. It looks as far-reaching as acquiring the higher consciousness did when I first started to get control. It is the round trip—the completing of the circle.

Betty: (Long pause.) I must try to tell you what I experienced just now in being unable to utilize the love force around me. I could not hold it condensed and shape it in any form, even though I took the most buoyant one of wings. I must explain this, because we've got to understand it—the pain of taking shape, the anguish of particularization. I feel almost agonizingly sensitized in my perceptions, and I know what the years ahead have in store for me in the strain of taking shape. I have no right to take more expansion. It would be like overfeeding, or massed wealth—something damaging to me. I've had my share of the raw material of eternal existence. I have been allowed for years to experience the rhapsody of higher life, but now I come willingly to suffer the pain of shaping one little verse from the great rhapsody.

Take a concrete example from our everyday lives. Let

219

us say we have decided that our days are going to be shaped in freedom of movement, unbarnacled. And suppose we have acquired the expansion of heart, and are trying to live it widely and glowingly and merrily. Now we come to the point: there is something more than that. If we stop there, it is almost a stagnation. We have got to be continually taking those very qualities of liberation and wide sympathy, and suffering the diminishments of our emotions that shape them into something needed in the world, something of universal appeal, something near to others.

Invisible: You have learned to approach the higher consciousness as the source and joy of life, to unify yourselves with it, and thus to intensify your spiritual beings to a higher pitch. You have also learned that from these moments of attunement something rare and fine can be brought back for use in daily life. But the thing you have not yet fully realized is that the *interpretation must be through ordinary material channels.* Therein lies the great secret of effective use. Heretofore so many classic examples of those illuminated by spirit have been unable to exhibit the fruits of the spirit in daily life. You *must* utilize the channels of earth life. You must not close them and seek to exhibit something artificially forced, and named spirituality.

Betty: So often people try to give it to others directly, but with the majority that won't work. I can't tell you just how it gets humanized to make it acceptable, but it seems to go out most successfully through all the nice laughing human sympathetic things.

Invisible: The individual who sits alone, even though thinking exaltedly, accomplishes little for his generation beyond exemplifying pure sublimity. The limitation of this method of spreading one's influence is its wastefulness in proportion to one's effort and intent. On the other hand, the same type of mind, capable of entering the stream of life, of participating in the trivial pleasures and interests and pastimes of his fellow beings, of amalgamating with their main purposes— which are their heart impulses, and not their surface minds—this person's influence is incalculable. His harmonious intent and radiating, perceptive interest in life touch countless lives beyond his vision.

The most effective obtainable association with one's fellow beings is to work at something together. That supplies the perfect condition for interchange and expression of vision and character and ability. That is, fortunately, the condition supplied to mankind in general. But "Society" lacks this great common cohesion, and at once it becomes too individualized, and has to cope with the artificialities of this perversion. The highest types in it adjust themselves according to their interests—musically, artistically, etc.—with enough general interchange to leaven each other. The lower reaches of Society strive to substitute with specializing games. Anything to afford a concrete vehicle of expression: that is the ultimate necessity.

And so I repeat: you must have bonds of genuine intense interest with your fellow beings. You *must* cultivate them, be proficient in them, if you are to achieve anything approaching the effectiveness of which you are capable.

(Pause.)

Betty: I am not going to talk much about it. But tonight I've visualized for myself the necessity for the pain of particularization—of taking from the beautiful raw material of life and continually shaping something. It is the zest and passion of creation's anguish. We've got to realize it as vividly and with as great an ardor as we have the expansion that liberates us from it.

Textbooks are not important except as they produce skillful human beings. Therefore personal usefulness has been the object of these teachings, more than the recording of techniques. Nevertheless we are starting this subject of communication, and for two reasons: 1, in order to give you long-delayed intellectual satisfaction; 2, in order to emphasize a warning.

The warning is this: in doing this work, do not grab hold of any force you are not sure of. If you opened an unregulated mind at a time like this, you would get a great rush of force that might hustle you anywhere. It sweeps the drifters into the dark shadows of conditions created by the strong destructive ones. If you would protect yourself from this, you must in general maintain yourself with a radio-active mind that is outgoing and definite, and not start ignorantly grabbing any stray impulses that may come along.

CHAPTER V

SUPERVISION

The ideas expressed in the chapter before this were thoroughly satisfactory to us. We are Occidentals, and Oriental quietism could never appeal to us. Sitting down and "emanating," or posing as Shining Examples just is not our nature. Along with most of our race, we prefer to *do* something.

So, far, however, our instructions included nothing specific to work on. To be sure, we had been admonished that we must use "material channels." But that, after all, was only a fuzzy generality. And as against that we had also been warned—and in no uncertain terms—against "considered acts" (intellectual), or "working it out by details." There was here a decided gap. About the only clue, at this time, was the statement that, "if this through process is acquired, it will keep open a channel through which inspiration will come for the necessary individual acts." That looked promising.

The promise was shortly to be fulfilled. In due time the Invisibles followed up their clue. The technical explanations, however, were based on certain theories previously advanced concerning the method of their communications through Betty. Therefore it is well to give the highlights of these here. The following excerpt is from the record of a "party," and therefore includes a bit of the entertaining background we often get. This time the Invisible was someone well known to all present.

Betty: What a strange way to work! He's throwing, like a javelin thrower. He's throwing it toward us, like a penetrating powerful current, like an electric vibration, sent out to pierce resistance. It's like segregating, by surrounding it, a portion of the dense, resisting material which is all about us.

(At this point, under Betty's direction, Stewart drew the following diagram:)

Betty: That is the way we are surrounded, magnetically contained. He does it so that he can control that enclosed portion. It can then be penetrated, much as the vacuum of a radio tube is penetrated by a broadcast.

Joe: Reducing the pressure against me is what I'm trying to get at. Surrounding you enables me to send the full force of a message: in ordinary transmission it is greatly diminished. My present work is, so to speak, to rarefy the atmosphere between us. By this system I'm trying to lessen the intervening obstruction.

Betty: Curious registration! It's *quite* like a radio tube: it's got to have its proper surrounding-atmosphere and insulation.

Joe: That's very nearly it. Briefly, crudely, roughly: the force exercised from this side is a kind of magnetic power. All of this force I can command I put into surrounding and insulating you. This sensitizes you, and your contribution is a species of magnetic response. This response of yours is vitally necessary, but the more magnetized you become the easier it is for you to give it.

I can't say I've made it very clear, but I do want you to realize there's a definite mechanism to it—it's not a vague, fuzzy, hit-or-miss thing. But if you could visualize, even vaguely, the process going on, it would be very, very helpful.

(We began to talk about Joe—some of his characteristics—as if he were not there.)

Betty: You talk about him as if he were in Podunk, and he's right here.

Stewart: That's true! We get the idea that this communication business is like talking over the phone: you put your hand over the receiver and make side remarks.

Joe: Thank heaven for that! It at least implies I'm not an Angelic Being. Guard against that reaction. We've got to watch out or you will de-humanize us. We don't want to become just precious memories.

Stewart: How do you see us?

Joe: I see you in our material—as Betty is seeing you now.

Betty: Come on, let's cook this up for them, Joe. I'll help you.

Stewart: Can you see me, Joe?

Joe: Now, isn't that the deuce!

Betty: Here we are, Joe and I, standing looking at you, and neither of us can explain how we do it!

Joe: How does a strong emotion come to you? Is it, or isn't it, reality? What does it look like? What's the shape of it? How do you know it is there?

Well then, how do I know *you're* there?

Stewart: I meant physical sight. If I set a marble rolling across the floor, would you see that?

Joe: It's just as easy to follow the marble rolling across the floor as can be; but I'm trying to make out the difference between the way I see it and the way you see it. I can't get it....

I don't *see* it; I *know* it.

Stewart: Can you enjoy your sitting-room at home, for example, and all the things that are in it, the way you used to?

Betty: He says he contains it. It's the difference between walking in a village and looking at it from a hill. You see it all at once, and not piecemeal.

(Betty's voice had been pitched unusually high, and at this point it broke.)

I *wish* you wouldn't make me squeak that way! You make me do such silly, exaggerated things; you push me so....

He doesn't use myself well.

Stewart: You ought to be more careful of her, Joe.

Joe: Am. But....

(Fits of laughter for a long time.)

Betty: He says I'm not the size he used to wear.

(Pause; sobering down.)

Let's tell them about the process, Joe: how you do it.

Joe: Suppose you had a sponge saturated with paint, and you poured gasoline through it. The gasoline would come through, but it would be a mixture; the paint representing your physical voice, the gasoline the ideas I am trying to get to you.

Roughly, that is what happens, once the thing gets going. But first must come a preparation. While you are in your ordinary consciousness, my ideas are separated from you by a state of non-absorption. It's like a drop of water on glass instead of blotting paper. To get by this I have to reckon first on a definite desire from your side. Without that there is the merest chance of success. Granted this desire, the preliminary preparation on my part is to hold off from you, temporarily, the pressure of conditions normal to your life. I raise the weight, something like heat dispelling cold. After that is lifted, it is like looking into a lighted room from the outside dark, or into the different element of an aquarium.

That is the first process—this surrounding you with an atmosphere of higher potentiality. Then registration is accomplished by means of the mating of our sensitized consciousness, superimposed: something like the making of a color print.

Betty: I am just like a photographic plate. The idea is there, and I expose myself to it until I feel I have a negative. Then I develop it and pass it on to you.

Joe: You see the whole thing starts with something you yourself create. If I could only get this forcibly enough to you! It should never be forgotten. Perhaps you will remember it better if you think of it as just like any of your other closer contacts. Take friendship, for example: you approach your real friends with exactly the same process of lightening pressures, of warmth in each other's atmospheres, of getting directly in touch with the intimate sides of them which are less recognized by the world in general. All this is a commonplace there: you take it for granted. But with us you sometimes forget.

In this particular kind of communication, of course, from then on it is a little different. It is something like learning another language so you can listen intelligibly. Each time you desire to travel beyond your present country you must say to yourself: Am I thinking and listening in the right language? Otherwise communication is hopeless.

While we are on the subject of communication, it might be well to point out that here is another attractive-looking blind-end trail. Too many of us forget that communication is merely a means, and not an end. The curious feel of the pencil moved under one's fingers by some outside agency; the mystery of talking by direct voice with an invisible intelligence summoned out of the depths of space—these are so fascinating that we are too prone to follow them solely for the sake of the undeniable thrill. There is the lure of fishing for distant radio stations; the novelty of a new toy; and in over-plus the high adventure of exploration. Also, sad to say, there is too often a subtle tickling of the ego that such as we are the chosen for such celestial attentions!

So important do these things seem, against our experience-background, that we are tempted to pursue them for themselves. We covet "occult powers," and we go after them. And the worst of it is that indubitably, if we do so, we shall get results. Oh, perfectly genuine results! But, unless at the same time we have learned what we are to do with those "powers," we shall suddenly find ourselves possessed of something we can neither use nor control. For if we "sit for psychic development," as the jargon has it, it is likely to be exactly as though a suckling should "sit for development of teeth"—and get them, to the discommoding of all concerned!

That does not mean we should Prussianize our natural interest and enthusiam in experiment. Zest is an oxygen necessary to the very life of new adventure. But here, as always, we must keep our proportions, and guard against rushing into things inappropriately. Consider, said the Invisibles, the leisurely growth of a child.

"Surrounding you," said they, "and pressing on you on every side, on every atom of you, are myriad manifestations of life. They would crush you in, if you did not possess the human machine's quality of resistance to them. The child is quite completely insulated at first. With each year his perceptions increase and he lets in more and more—but *only as much as he can happily control.* That must also be the rule, if you are to keep your balance, in psychic development."

Granted, you say: but how are we to assure this? The best answer was given at the very start of this journey: it lies in distinguishing clearly between the ultimate aim and the by-product. No degree of devotion *to the ultimate aim* can injure us; but the same intensity directed toward a by-product can easily blow out our fuses. The Invisibles presented this alternative very neatly.

Said they: "When one works consistently toward any primary aim, there results legitimately and automatically from that work certain accompanying by-products. These are often desirable and useful, but there is always danger of mistaking some desirable by-product for the ultimate aim. Energies are then directed intensively toward this new, false aim, from which results disaster. In a pursuit as richly flowering as this supreme task of inner development, these by-products are naturally both more numerous and more desirable than in most pursuits. Therefore those susceptible to glitter will here be more easily deflected—especially by the so-called psychic powers, which are a prime example of a by-product."

Here is the point, then, in a nutshell: the aim of these or any other worth-while teachings is the acquisition, *not* of psychic powers, but of a *manner of living.* Toward this ultimate all our searching and efforts, all our

228

expedients and experiments and "exercises," must be directed. A method of life, that is what we are to learn.

That in the process we do make acquisition of ease and serenity and health; that we do gain new insight, new comfort and happiness—and even, incidentally, certain definite new powers; we can accept thankfully. But ordinarily these should be automatically accompanying rewards, and not ends in themselves. And, if we do go after them as ends in themselves, if we do attempt this excursion into higher consciousness with any predominant idea of getting more vitality, or "psychic power," or personal happiness—or even with so apparently laudable an ambition as conscientious preparation for eternity—we are almost certain to miss out. These things may be added unto us; but as a rule, only in corollary.

For the most part, the Invisible were reticent concerning the detailed technique of communication. The idea seemed to be that they did not want to risk misconceptions which might get in the way. Consequently our understanding of it was built up only little by little, mostly from casual fragments in discourses along other lines. The following is typical of this kind of thing. We had been discussing a certain striking idea, trying to determine who had "originated" it, so that we could give "credit" to its author.

Invisible: When a person says something true he isn't saying anything he invented. He just gives a certain shape and character to it, that's all. You can't invent truth. Anything that's true, even if it seems suddenly true, was always true. One of the things you've got to get rid of is the idea that truth was invented by, or belongs to, anybody in particular.

Very often even the ordinary thoughts you have are

not strictly "your own." For instance, you'll have what you think are random thoughts: where do you suppose they come from? It's funny to spend half a day yelling in a fellow's ears, and then hear him say, "I just had a nice little funny thought." Or you lie there, getting ready to work with us, and say, "This is just myself thinking." You *know* it is. But it isn't; not once in a thousand times!

Stewart: I'm getting more and more diffident about claiming that I think or say *anything* myself!

Invisible: Well, there's no use in feeling *that* way about it, either. We very often divert certain masses of things toward your consciousness—yes. But, except in certain special circumstances, like the present, it is not too common that we impress a specific rounded idea upon you. We divert to you a certain mass or class of impression, and as much of it flows through your actual consciousness as your individual capacity or ability of *that moment* selects. So it really *is* your thought, after all! We have just given you a favorable opportunity for that thought.

The foregoing, of course, is a broad statement. There are many times, especially when there is a close bond, when a specific thought can be inserted. But the general mechanism of influence is just this broad diverting process of mass, from which you take, so to speak, magnetically.

In the very beginning, naturally, like most novices, we inclined to the belief that the strictly controlled type of "dictation" must be the most effective method of communication; more "definite," and therefore "accurate."

For certain very special types of work, this may very likely be true; though the scope is definitely limited,

230

and the accuracy often only apparent. But for general use, as we learned in due course, the "dictation" method is actually the least effective. In fact the higher the type of work—particularly from the point of view of the translator's personal development—the less the Invisibles impose exact control!

Because of this, Betty was constantly directed toward greater and greater self-reliance. The following is a fairly recent fragment, that gives an interesting glimpse into her later technical process:

Betty: (After a pause.) They are showing me a very advanced method of reaching us. A special kind of adjustment is involved: the sort of thing the specialists over here use to look at us. It shows our world very dark—black. Here and there are spots of glow or phosphorescence from the more developed among us. The glow comes, not so much from any light of our own, as from the decay or passing off of the lower parts of us, the undeveloped parts.

Now I am taking the point of view of a very highly developed person on this side, one of the really great Radiant Ones. If I were such a one, and wanted to help someone with the phosphorescent glow in the darkness, how would I go about it? Why, I think I would just come close and contemplate him, and so bring the effect of my radiation on him.

And what would be the result of that? First of all it would burn away or melt away the external dull crust, exposing the core of his reality. And that core would then reflect the light of my radiation, thus becoming visible to the man. It would not glow of itself, but it could now reflect light from me; and that would show that man to himself—make himself visible to him.

Do you see? It was all dark to him before, but now he can see himself because of this reflected light, and can perceive his needs and lacks and all that. And then while the glow is on him—and *only* then—he can write to himself about it, or talk to himself about it, in detail, just what he needs. But all *I* have done is to bring my radiation to him.

Stewart: Is that anything like the way the Invisibles work with us now?

Betty: Yes. Enough of this psychic work, this companionship, has been done, so that now they dare allow us to work more independently. To a certain extent we ourselves have learned to take the universal force. We do this imperfectly perhaps, but at our highest moments we at least realize the possibility of taking it entirely on our own. Therefore to say that what we receive is a direct utterance or gift from our Invisibles is no longer an accurate description of the process—however fosteringly it may be watched and conditions provided for its functioning, and however much we may feel the stimulus and affection and beneficence of an influence.

It is important to understand this. We no longer have copybook words given us. We experiment in expressing our own ideas in our own words. Any expectation of the old method, except in occasional emergencies, is a retrogression doomed to disappointment. This is a much higher and more secure form of communication—one that will be maintained on this line, progressively, for the rest of our lives.

In the course of time Betty's method seems to have arrived at a kind of equilibrium. What the future has in store, of course, cannot be foreseen, but the following describes her present approach.

Betty: First I ease my body into pleasant memories. I lull it to comfort. I think of the wind in the pines; or feel the sun's warmth—perfect physical peace and enjoyment; entirely concerned with my own body. Life surrounding me is nonexistent. It is as if a trap door were closed. I am within myself: content.

Slowly, in that content, there forms an interest, a desire to expand. I do not define any more: I *feel*. I feel that there is a secret exit; something awaiting exploration; something highly desirable and exciting. It lies in a different direction from that which I entered by, and closed off. Something can flow into me, and I can flow out to it with the same comfort with which I relaxed the body; only within the comfort is desire and latent strength, release into a well-being which I cannot define in words. It is an essence of life, not to be put down in lesser terms.

For the moment I am quite oblivious to active life. Creeping into this communion is a new energy; an energy which is unconscious of arms and legs, of hands, of ordinary senses. It is a perception which illuminates itself. That is, it brings out into the spotlight of awareness, in more or less complete vision according to the strength of the light, whatever it holds steadily and interestedly—whatever it stimulates itself, or is stimulated, to hold steadily and interestedly.

Sometimes I merely enjoy the ebb and flow. It is like music, a natural response of tones. Then in my contentment I feel a pattern forming. I watch, amused; interested, as at a movie performance. I watch to be sensitive and ready to pick up the first delicate impressions that come. I pick them up like a dance to music in time with the subtleties; for if I impose my own clumsiness of rhythm, I strain myself and fumble into stupidities.

Then again, through this same adjustment, after an artistically suitable time for establishing myself, I try gently but firmly to present deferentially a pattern of my own. I introduce a motif into the music, something of a quaint little composition of my own; and if it pleases they catch the refrain and amplify it into rich variations. And then, still amusedly, I give myself to this until I am practiced enough and strong enough myself to repeat it back to you through all the different transformations to our rough-hewed words.

That is the mystic method; the surest, the safest, the most accurate and skillful. There are many other methods, some with greater facility; but not self-induced and under self-control.

The sparkling radiance of sunshine on water, of lights meeting glass and silver, of any illumination capable of being reflected in some responsive surface, is not a beauty complete in the nature of the illumination itself. That has only potential radiance until it meets the thing that combines with it and produces the actuality of radiance.

Wisdom is man's hard-won heritage of experience, plus the interplay of the higher consciousness, accepted even if uncomprehended. Precipitation of these joint forces through the intellect is called inspiration, and is the attribute of genius.

CHAPTER VI

TECHNIQUE

Every writer worth his salt is familiar with the fact that he, as a deliberately planning person, has but a minor part in his work. Most of it, and the best of it, is done "instinctively," "subconsciously," with "inspiration," the choice of the word depending upon his bias of belief. So well publicized is this phenomenon as to writers that there is small utility in laboring the point here. But that it obtains as to all other men in all other callings is not so well acknowledged. Nevertheless that is the way all the worthwhile forward-moving work of the world is accomplished. And, pinned down to honesty, any business man, professional man, statesman, will admit it. "Follow your hunch," as a phrase, has become part of the language. And as practical advice it needs little addition. "Welcome your hunch, and examine it," perhaps. Then, nine times in ten, you will follow it.

Now as a professional writer I, the senior author of this book, had of course long been familiar with all that. I do not remember being so highfalutin' as to think of myself as "inspired"; but I did know that when one got going, in suitable mood, things came without conscious summoning. All I had to do was to be alert for them, and sort them out, and appropriately utilize them. The suitable mood was essential: but I had scant patience with those who "wrote only on inspiration," as they called it. Such people did a lot of lazing around doing nothing, waiting for the said inspiration to hunt them up. And then the intervals between visits had a tendency to lengthen. I "wrote only on inspiration" also, but my own experience was that if I kept office hours, sat at my desk anyway, mood or no mood, inspiration or no inspiration, those intervals tended to shorten. In other words the mood could be induced.

Such were to me the workaday conditions of my job—of any writer's job. If anybody had then told me that we were close kin to those who, from a base of religion, superstition, or just plain insanity, talk of "divine guidance," I would have hooted.

But this present teaching, carried to the point at which we have now arrived in this book, gave me pause. Some of these other people might be overwrought and extreme, but were they not acting in the same chain of causation? And when I sat down at my desk, at 8:00 A.M., was I not doing my ritual of invocation no different *in essence*—though vastly in outward seeming—from the sacraments, mysticisms or plain abracadabra I had thought so alien? And might not the whole be ordered into something approaching conscious control?

It began to look that way. For one thing Betty's teaching seemed to imply that all these various manifestations were actually the functioning of a specific faculty—something quite as definite as our physical senses. Heretofore it had not been to us as palpable as these, simply because it dealt with things which ordi-

236

narily we do not recognize, and of which therefore we are unaware.

This faculty Betty had made use of from the beginning, in all her work in communication, but more or less unconsciously. Now it was presented to her more as something to be used independently; again in one of her symbolic experiences.

Betty: (After a long interval.) I'm exchanging my usual senses for those of a higher order....

Why, it's kind of *sight*—a feeling of sight! Very cautiously, they're trusting me with a little. It's just like light where it has been dark before; like a room where you've groped, and then found and turned on the light.

Invisible: It's the sense you discover by union of direct inspiration with your human mind. This combination, persisted in, generates a kind of sight.

Betty: I can't see anything with it yet. It's just a kind of pathfinding sight now. I am not allowed to see things with it, but I can find my way. It is just a penetrating shaft of light now, like a searchlight ahead of me....

How else could I find my way, if I didn't generate that? How else could I know which way to go through that silently clanging machinery?

Invisible: With greater inspiration and greater mental capacity you can extend that shaft of light. In time you can also extend it around you, instead of just straight ahead. Everything, every step, has to be balanced that way. Penetration: then expansion to proportion.

Betty: I'm beginning to see the application. Suppose you get into that clanging factory, that awful place of discordant elements—that's the world of limited sight where you can't understand values—and get confused over issues. You are in this world and you cannot tell the greatest good from the present expediency: you can't distinguish the right thing to do. Instead of trying to fight through with your intellect, you retire to the higher consciousness and begin your inner generation. This produces a shaft of power and light which you can turn on your problem. Then you see clearly, and easily find your solution.

(Pause.)

I keep talking of *seeing*, but that doesn't really express this higher sensing process at all. It is more as if my whole body were a kind of sight. Feeling and sensation come nearer to it: I perceive with my sensation. I see with my mind and feelings quite distinctly, in a kind of direct absorption of the realities around me. It is hard to make sense of it in words, but the main thing is that you are not at all dependent on any one little channel of information. You could just as well call it listening. It is what Joe was talking about when he said that if you keep still and listen, things will always explain themselves. It is as if something drew near to you, and formed, and revealed itself—something that holds itself at a distance when you don't listen.

I wish there were a better word for it—this perceptive stillness which pierces all barriers, dissolves them, and releases you into such breathless vistas.

Invisible: The attempt to describe this faculty inevitably gives the impression of something vague and indeterminate. Actually it is nothing of the sort. Nor is the acquisition of knowledge by its aid a hit-or-miss affair—a mere unregulated absorption of indiscriminate impressions. In practice you are magnetically attracted toward whatever you are in need of at the moment—there is a natural pulsing toward it. And then this particular thing begins actively to seep into you: an intensive soaking-up process. It acts on you constantly as you go along, and reaches every bit of you, like any other permeating action. In contrast to our mere verbal instruction, it is like being out in a fog instead of just being sprinkled in spots. That is the way you acquire knowledge here.

Betty: The odd part of it is that the effect is not of some strange overpowering magic. It is just a perfectly ordinary magic of illumination. And even the illumination comes to you in quite an ordinary fashion—mostly through comprehension of how to utilize all the lesser laws pertaining to the obstructions ahead.

But the important thing to remember about it is that the *inner generation must come first;* because the illumination of method follows as its result, and we are so apt to stray when we study too closely the methods alone.

(Pause.)

I wish I knew who was teaching me today: he's such a wise feeling-hearted person. He had such a tremendous fund from which to give, yet he gave it so cautiously, so cleverly, so painstakingly. It didn't seem exactly like one person alone, either, but more like a combination: somebody doing the reading from someone else's book, as you might say.

Not long after this the Invisibles undertook more exactly to define the connection of all this with our ordinary faculties.

Betty: I am so changed today: something is happening—so changed today! I cannot understand how I can be so determinedly and vigorously *I,* and yet at the same time be so filled and possessed with this great force that overflows and surrounds everything. My mind won't push to it....

(Pause.)

How astounding! I have been taken apart, haven't I, these past few years: very carefully and cautiously separated, for the sake of developing certain parts difficult of access in my ordinary life. Now I am being put together

239

again. That part they wanted to develop has caught up. There was danger of letting it get ahead of the others, so now I am being assembled....

(Pause.)

I understand the need for reassembling, all right. What I am struggling for now is to get just where the human brain belongs in the combination. Up to now they have said so little about *mentality*. Here's where it comes in and finds its supplementing place.

Invisible: Simultaneously with the higher consciousness must be exercised the intellectual functions, now established in subservience. Each function must be duly exercised. From now on you must beware of separation.

Betty: *I* think they've been treating my mind like a poor relation, making me neglect it and sniff at it when I really didn't want to! I'm *much* more comfortable about it, now that it's got official recognition.

Invisible: The intellect is a marvelous mechanism, and must be highly respected. It is wonderfully effective in combination with the inner self, but alone it is blind and poverty-stricken. Its proper functioning is when it works with humility as a subordinate—a kind of valuable, indispensable secretarial department. It is then possible to bring to bear on problems the whole mind—the great, invisible, submerged foundations of all thought, as well as the lesser, if more evident, part that deals with the earth details.

Betty: I'm getting to understand it a little now. On the one hand there is the inner self; and then there's our intellect, like a wonderful machine. The machine must be worked by the other wiser guiding consciousness. If left unrelated or unguided it is ineffectual—even destructive.

Invisible: Utilization of the mental faculties without the aid of the inner self is always dry, desiccated, unvitalized—however astounding the achievement. On the other hand, it also is difficult or impossible for the creative power of the higher consciousness to act on your world, unless you make of yourselves effective channels through which it can function. For this purpose the intellect is an indispensable tool—you cannot work without it. It forms the point of contact with earth life—the actual point.

(Pause.)

Betty: You remember how bewildered I was when I first got into this other world, and how I had no faculties with which to function and work in it? Well, it is just the same with this higher force when it is brought back here and has to push its way through our crowded life. It would be equally confused and groping and helpless if it were not for the trained physical faculties. There must be mentality that knows how to use this force, how to apply it, to make it more useful.

Invisible: Properly regulated, the intellect is like a diamond-pointed cutting tool for the vast spiritual power which it cannot comprehend, but which it can acknowledge and be directed by—can learn dependence on for its strength and purposes. Its fine adjustments, so beloved and desired by you all, then become like the hands of the inner being, to be trained in co-ordination with their spiritual director.

(Pause.)

Betty: Curious how that works out practically. If all your attention is on a strong vision of the spirit of a thing—anything—your intellect steps in like an obedient, well-trained servant, and carries out the labor of producing the vision.

Invisible: Your picture is good, but do not let it mislead you into passivity. Do not get the idea that *you yourself* are merely an efficient tool attached to a power mechanism. It is only your intellect that is the power

241

driven tool, which you as a skilled workman must still manipulate. Your own position is more that of the artist planning a design to be carried out by this carving tool. The artist has in himself the potentiality of a great many designs or purposes from which he may choose. This choice, in association with forces capable of carrying it forward, is entirely yours to do. The part of the greater consciousness is first to inspire and then to supervise your creative contribution.

Betty: I see: it isn't like just being led blindly. It's more like following a compass.

Invisible: That is better; but in following your compass always remember that your destination is a definite thought form, arrived at by aid of the best information, analysis and judgment you can command. That must always be the first objective. But also do not forget that after your greatest efforts have been made mentally, the result should again be referred to the higher consciousness for criticism and completion—like an offering which you hold above your head for judgment as to its worthiness, in full confidence that your best will be accepted and amplified.

All this, however, is more in the nature of detail. The central factor remains the *absolute necessity for making, through your human faculties, channels for action.* Your life, accompanied by spiritual power gained from association with the higher consciousness, may be beautiful and inspiring as an example, but it cannot be as fruitful as intended unless fully developed through your own intellectual perception of how best to apply the power.

Of course, the warmth of the spirit is a permeating atmosphere, surrounding and glorifying even the most trivial human acts. And there is no doubt that it accomplishes much in harmonizing those with whom it comes in contact. But you can possess this power in full force only when it focuses through the lens of your intellect.

Always the great escape of your spirit into realization of the Scheme above your present range of vision must be fully exercised. And never should you neglect the examining of life through the more powerful lens of the higher consciousness. But then you must take the inspiration you acquire in these moments of vision, and apply it as vigorously as possible through the mental equipment that gives the practical application. That part must not be neglected, for unmistakably it is your present field of action.

The idea seemed to sum up about as follows:

Generate power by association with the higher consciousness. From the vantage in this association clearly envision the end in view. Concentrate on that. Do not search for details of the means of accomplishing the end. That merely confuses, and is unnecessary. They will automatically present themselves if the aim is held long enough and steadily enough for clarification; and may then be seized and utilized by the ordinary faculties. Last of all, when the thing is made, take it once more to the power house, the higher consciousness, for judgment.

This formula fitted my own experience. That is the way any successful writing, that is not hack work, comes into being.

But the Invisibles were not satisfied to leave it at that.

Invisible: All things in the universe constantly flow through you, awaiting only your choice and arrestment. Music, for instance, is all around you, like electricity, needing for its manifestation only the apparatus for trapping it. The room you sit in is filled with music, though you are deaf to it. But anybody with the proper equipment can pick it out of the air, just as you pick electricity out of the air. There is very little difference: in either case one works to co-operate with unseen forces. Only with the music, in place of metals and vacuums and dynamos, one utilizes intention, nerve relaxation, expansion of mind—the spiritual tuning which puts into operation the magnetic attraction of music.

I do not want to complicate the picture with further details, but the same principle applies equally to every other creative field. Of course, if he so desires, any human being can remain unaware of these forces which are constantly passing through him and in which he is immersed. But also, in greater or less degree, it is perfectly possible for anyone voluntarily to attune himself with them. Fortunately mankind in general does this, to an extent, without understanding it. It is the unrecognized commonplace of all successful achievement. But conscious, voluntary tuning, to catch the harmonies of inspiration, should be a matter for *intensive education*. Only in that way will you become really effective filters for the higher consciousness.

In fact, spiritual porosity....

Betty: How absurd! Suddenly my body doesn't exist for me except as pores. All sorts of beautiful, warm, pulsing things are coming through and saturating me. I feel like a lily-pad stem!

Invisible: Spiritual porosity is the one absolute requirement if you are to tap genius instead of mere cleverness—which is the tour de force of your unaided efforts. Too great development on the intellectual side does not admit the need of this absorption. It is looked on as dangerous to logic. But could it be developed to the point where it would nourish the intellect, then we would have man as he is intended to be—as he is

244

now in moments of devotion to ideals.

Everyone who achieves true greatness has discovered to some degree the secret of this admission of nourishment. In fact, the great secret of all progress is to let the universal force continually flow through you; as often as possible to clear moments in your life in which to circulate it intensively through your being, stimulating mind and body and every part of you; and then, nourished by it, to let your mental faculties plan its utilization. Clarity of aim, untroubled persistence, flexibility in replacing that aim by higher and higher forms as wisdom unfolds—these are the intellectual aids to creative power. The creative impulse itself, from the superconscious side, once it has been adjusted to the intellect will discover its own detailed ways and means.

Remember this especially whenever you go astray or suffer from diminishments and bafflements. Uncertainty resides on the surface of life; surety lives at its core. Consequently when things go wrong, abandon all contemplation of your problem in detail and recall your activities to the center of your being. There nourish, refresh and replenish yourself through the entrance of the vital essence; attracting it, allowing it to circulate comfortably over a long enough period to evaporate all the miasmatic indecision of the fog. Your vitalized intuitional faculties restored, you will then go ahead confidently in the right direction, surprised at the simplicity of the problem under your healthy invigorated illumination.

(Pause.)

Stewart: Your scheme is clear enough, but I think a lot of people might balk at the "humility and subordination" aspect of it. The modern idea of freedom and rugged individualism runs counter to all that.

Invisible: One of the finest things in the world today

245

is the desire for freedom—but in its name there is so much blind and destructive effort! Freedom is not isolation: freedom is self-generalship in harmonious action with the forces about you. And the more you ally yourself with the higher consciousness, the more you become aware of greater forces to be co-operated with in order to gain still greater freedom.

Of course it is perfectly *possible* to go at it the other way around. One can work independently through trained mental activities, which finally by detailed comprehension must exhaust their limited area and so extend their boundaries to include higher forms of research. In time, this minute, painstaking dissection will inevitably lead into comprehension of wholes, but it is a comparatively ineffective method of entering the state of wisdom. That is best accomplished when things are first seen whole, and then the application is sought in detail.

Betty: We are going at things in the slow and laborious way when we work from this end with the little tools of the mind. What you want to do is to associate yourself first with the greater powers. It is so much easier to accomplish things if you have established this connection. It is like having the tide with you. Then the working of the details is automatic. You have your plan, your superior power, and it makes its own detailed manifestation. The other way you are working backward—you are making details before you have your plan.

Invisible: You cannot work at detail effectively until you have the big general scheme. If you just build up brick by brick, it is only when the structure is finished that you see wherein you should have worked toward seemingly inaccessible ideas of beauty and greater harmony. Accordingly it is much better to get in touch with the general plan first, even if only vaguely, and let

246

the whole shape itself ahead of—or at least along with—the minute part, the moment's work. The most satisfactory adjustment is always when there is a healthy flow between the vastly removed ideal, and the otherwise futile and absurd effort of the coral-building insect. No feeling of the uselessness of effort can ever come to one who has a great, almost unattainable vision with which to refresh himself....

One sees everywhere the results of harmoniously lived days: the tiny weak baby grown into the splendid athlete, the little acorn and the great oak. Everywhere one observes the effect of automatic, unconscious adjustment to higher laws controlling our evolution. Why not, then, decide to live up to our best potentialities, by giving conscious, painstaking, voluntary cooperation with the highest reaches of our mentality? The greatest obstruction to the healthy flow of the higher power is in those who will not definitely and consciously acknowledge any purposeful, constructive cosmic intelligence. The lack of that acknowledgment turns them adrift, as it were, and puts them solely on their own, to work brick by brick in confusion and doubt.

(Pause.)

Betty: I am diminishing; returning; darkening....I am set down gently.

"No vision should ever have a wall instead of a horizon," said the Invisibles; and in accordance they never permitted us to feel that any of the trails along which they directed us would come to an abrupt end. When we had gone as far on it as we could, it still led on, fading slowly into a distance of infinite possibilities ahead.

Like all the others, the present trail eventually reached its vanishing point. The following is its vista into the future:

247

Betty: Such a big step! Never to work alone. A deliberate hookup before every action: the accomplishment of that is the end and purpose of one's whole life. It is so simple and yet so tremendous—just like an electrical hookup.

Before I start anything I must drop my consciousness into place as a link between the Purpose I do not understand, and the little act of which I am master. It is the definite awareness of this hookup and the practice of it that makes it work, lets in the power. It is just a workaday natural action—my two hands directed by my spirit. If that were an accomplished habit, there would be no necessity for wrong or puzzlement. I would just say to Unknown Purpose: "I am ready when you are," and keep a steady confidence in the purpose at hand; and in due course it would be accomplished better than I could plan it.

Invisible: The entire secret is to make your hookup *every time*, before you get into action in minutiae and routines. There is nothing really new in this. The only clarification is the simple yet amazing thought that the law of empowerment depends on utilizing this hookup *for every separate act*. (Pause.)

Betty: This is the next great step. Until we accomplish it, not much more will be given. As I look into the future there doesn't seem to be so much emphasis on these verbal records: it is more a utilization of what has already been given. I can see the simple things we are to work with—just commonplace things to be done in a spiritual way.

Invisible: This does not mean that we have reached the limit of our possibilities. There still remains an endless amount of desirable information waiting to be precipitated concerning the detailed utilization of the higher consciousness. But first you must learn to work more consistently with your hookup.

248

A mere fostering or sending forth of undifferentiated harmonious influences from the heart batteries is a comparatively simple matter. That inevitably and unerringly reaches the corresponding life principles in your subject, and unfolds them for him quite naturally and safely. But the use of projective mentality to help another by means of your own detailed selection is always a risk. You are at once confronted by the problem of how best to create assimilable thought form without imposing undue personal restrictions. The thing you offer must be abstract enough to give freedom to the one you desire to help, and at the same time vivid enough to be utilizable as a strengthening of his own creative faculty. It is a very subtle balance to strike, and in it lie grave dangers of harming the very one you want to help. A misplaced intensity of the limited mind is so easily substituted for intensity of the heart, which knows the higher laws. Then, inevitably, you fall into the error of particularizing merely your own personal desires and limited perceptions. And once you begin that, you are actually restricting still further the very person you wish to free!

This is not intended to discourage, but merely to give a glimpse of the problems and difficulties ahead. Actually the more detailed administration can be attempted with reasonable safety, *provided your projection is made in the vehicle of affection.* It then has no sustained power to restrict.

This subject is tremendous. Only through years of experiment and practice can laws be proved. It is the entire next grade of life—the technique of the spiritual functions.

Today I have made a discovery. It is an age-old thing we are already supposed to know all about, but it must be cut and polished like a diamond so it has a new character and a new capacity for reflecting light. It is the fact that you can go another step beyond the spiritual expansion that exists only in moments of especial adjustment and inspiration, and make them ordinary everyday moments. It isn't just an old platitude: it is a law of fulfillment. It is a cycle, a completion of growth. Unless we can absorb this ordinary life we are living, and control ourselves in it so that at will it becomes spiritual and we enter the spiritual heart of it— unless we can adjust that now and here and in this life, then we have not fulfilled the law for which we were created, have not finished the cycle, completed the task. We have been too stupid to get the reward, and have only taken the work.

CHAPTER VII

NEW TERRITORY

Up to this time it had seemed to us as though the trail we were following led directly out into the remote regions of consciousness. But now, suddenly, we realized that actually it was not a straight line at all. It was a curve, returning us inevitably to the common-places of daily life. In fact, when we looked far enough back along this trail, we saw that it was more than a simple curve: it was a spiral. The instruction which had been given us in the early days, and which was later assembled to make up *The Betty Book*, completed the first turn of this spiral. The later teaching, which we are considering here, merely covered the very same ground, but in a higher phase. And as in our elementary work, the final arc of the curve led us quietly to our own dooryard.

Most of this later material, this "technique of the spiritual functions," has come to us in a manner somewhat different from the foregoing, and therefore is not appropriate here. But certain indispensable pointers concerning the resistances and difficulties of everyday life were given to Betty herself. This aspect of the teaching was introduced, as usual, by a general survey.

Betty: If you could imagine an immense plain at night that has been used as a battlefield, a devastated area; that is what man has done to his spiritual potentialities. Right on the horizon is this glow I want to get to—a steady light. On the other side is the wonderful vision of the civilization of the future. And here I am. I've seen what it ought to be, and now I've got to help do the whole area that way. The question is, how am I to go about it?

(Pause.)

I have a clue, but it is hard to explain. I see certain very simple elements—separate things, individual entities. And then I see those same elements joined together, made into a compound of a much higher order. This compound has all sorts of possibilities that the separate individuals haven't got. I see that clearly enough. What I don't understand is how I can help bring about the compound....

Invisible: By way of fumbling into the subject: How should these simple elements become convinced of the desirability of the higher compound? That is the real problem. Once convinced of this, they would enthusiastically lend themselves in combination with others to produce it, in order that they might share in the beneficial attributes of the resulting whole. Your task, then, is to help demonstrate this desirability, beginning with very simple practices, indulged in habitually enough to carry conviction.

Actually a start has already been made at producing

this compound on a world wide scale. This thing spreading around the world—this sudden awareness of the lower rungs of society, uniting in a determination to lift themselves to a higher one—is the first manifestation of what we are discussing. But its appearance causes such violent reaction, such misunderstood interpretations, as to bring risk of complete defeat to the cause. That is the ferment inevitable to the first precipitation of this consciousness.

(Pause.)

Betty: As I look at it, I don't see how in the world it is going to be possible for *individuals* to want this unification. We stand stiff-necked and apart in instantaneous and habit-hardened oppositions.

Invisible: That is always the first misunderstanding of this new influence. Each entity is trying passionately *not* to be changed. In his fear of that, he destroys blindly. That is the resistance to be overcome, and that is the reason so minute an amount of influence can be sent at a time. A greater amount would precipitate the earth into chaos. Remember this always in administering from above to below.

Betty: I see the danger of not reducing, all right. So *many* visioned people have projected themselves to the detriment of their cause. They antagonized instead of allying.

Invisible: There is a fashion element here, which is a good safeguard. Social usages are quite right in forbidding our boring each other with heavy topics or indecent exposure of one's inner life. The first rule should be never to go around indecently, sloppily baring your innermost self to people.

(Pause.)

Betty: Isn't it funny how I see things! On the one hand there are all these big realities we are bored by. And then there's the curiously restricted body, so inadequate to receive more than a trickle through. It seems too bad that I'm capable of contemplating those realities, and then can't take more of them back. They've all got to be so tremendously reduced....

I look in the face of big things, like honor and confidence and sympathy and things like that; and then I've got to adjust them to an ant hill. How *would* you introduce them to an ant hill? Oh *my!* It is so hard to attract ants' attention—you can't get their minds off what they are doing! All I want is their attention: I could connect up if I could get that.

Anyone who has in any way become interested in "occult" or "mystical" matters knows the back-kick to which one is liable if he tries to pass this interest on to others. He can avoid that particular form of laceration, of course, by just keeping still about it—which is generally the best thing to do. But when it comes to the actual *use* of the principles which these subjects inevitably convey, it is no longer possible to sidestep so conveniently. We are then faced with the alternative of abandoning altogether what we believe to be our best course; or of evolving some practical, and not too vulnerable method of adapting it to an imperfect world. As to the latter the Invisibles had some illuminating suggestions.

Invisibles: In seeking to apply the higher consciousness to daily life, the first thing we must learn is to take for granted the usual resistances and obstacles encountered in any paths except those established and much travelled. When we are very young we foolishly expect gangway for ourselves anywhere, and we thrash around in fine style when we are jostled by others possessing exactly this same idea. But with more experience in life and heightened vision, we accept the ob-

253

structions as part of the game of living. This is a very important step in progress, for the first application of wisdom is to accept opposition so in its entirety, so completely, that thereafter not one speck of attention power is ever wasted on it, except for the intellectual appraisement of its strength and the planning for control of its effect.

The most important factor in this control is arranging to work from a safe insulation. Otherwise you will be constantly in danger of being drawn into the sphere of influence of the opposition and captured by disharmony. This principle is not a new thing. In your accustomed routine you often utilize destructive forces—such as dynamite, for instance—without hesitation, because of the mastery your knowledge and skill give you over them. This knowledge and skill constitute a species of insulation, which keeps you from becoming entangled in the sphere of influence of these destructive forces.

With difficult and destructive personalities it should be exactly the same. Take, for instance, somebody who is cock-sure of his own little universe—who is intellectually mind-proud of the content of human knowledge. Or, hardest of all to resist, the rollicking, amused, raconteur type: the loveable, charming stand-patters who are supplying the needed uneffortful vacationing atmosphere. Their function is perfectly good: we all need it. But one guards one's aspirations for the stars from them. One enjoys them as one does puppies or babies and such things, and guards one's self against them.

Now, your insulation can be of two kinds: negative and positive, characterized by the drawing-back person and the going-out person. In the past we have instructed you only as to the negative aspect—the retirement to your inner fortress. That conception was the

254

best we could convey with the force of illumination it was possible to use on you at that time. And it still holds good—but only to point the way to that other insulation which makes of yourself a sphere of influence stronger than the ones around you. That is a positive insulation—one in which you take the initiative; not a withdrawal.

This principle, also, is not a new thing: you have always used it in some degree without knowing it. Look, with critical dispassionate eye, on yourself as presented on the average to the world. How much do you register the impress and reflection of others; and how much do you register on and impress them? This is a very simple criterion of how much you are already using this primary creative capacity.

Betty: I'm beginning to understand it now. It looks something like keeping a natural, healthy manner in a sick room. You just maintain vigor in each directed thought.

Invisible: The waterfall sweeps clean the mind contemplating it: its refreshing, misty spray claims the beholder in a temporary waterfall-companionship. Likewise the sun expands and evaporates the contractions and isolations of the body. In just this way the power of the higher consciousness extends its influence. It controls by blanketing the opposition with its own quality.

Betty: That's very amusing; the body does that. It surrounds and isolates disharmonies, rendering them innocuous. Oysters do it, too, in making pearls. Lots of things in nature do it. They just capture and overcome any smothering, irreconcilable bit of trouble with a blanket of health wrapped around it. It is one of the very best ways of dealing with these spots. They are to be found everywhere, but if you can't absorb or transmute or eliminate them, you can always blanket them

255

in this way. I can't do it myself, but outflung selves can.

Invisible: A real outflung self is of such superior happiness that it is much less contaminable by world infections. Its resistance can be raised, just as bodily resistance is raised. You know what the comfort of physical health radiation is, but you cannot imagine the joy of true spiritual health. It is strange that people do not want it—try for it. Coin of great value is offered them, and they prefer a penny of their own mint.

Later on the Invisibles had more to say on this subject of meeting opposition. Apparently it is one of the fundamentals with which we have to deal.

Betty: (After a pause.) I have been studying the possibilities of protecting ourselves by projection. It is a very far-reaching subject....

(Pause.)

One positive fact: throughout the universe there's a great current of absolute stability, progressing force— call it what you please. Around it, below it is a sea of related living bits, representing all conditions of progress toward conscious unity with this great current. How they got that way I don't know; but they represent all the resistances of life—the calumnies, opposing activities, ponderous masses of ignorance, willful sluggards....

Now it worried and puzzled and discouraged me at first to know how I could cope with so much surrounding wrack and misdirected energy. It seemed so hopeless for me to set my aspirations against them. Then I remembered that as long as I can keep my volition magnetized to the point of unity with this great current, it finds the way for me through clarity of vision and revelation of the obstructions. Endowed with power

256

through association with it, I comprehend directions to take and find my way. Paying the penalties of the contact: oh yes! Outwardly damaged, perhaps; but inwardly unscathed and strengthened.

Invisible: In using this method of self-protection there is really only one serious danger: depletion of your supply of power. As water evaporates under the influence of the sun, so does the absorbing quality of world life diminish your spiritual supply. Therefore the first principle to keep in mind is the constant uninterrupted renewing of power. Have complete confidence in the power house, of which you are the distributor. Its force must be constantly maintained. Do not enter the lists depleted of this vital force.

Evaporation of force is so subtly accomplished that you may not always recognize your depletion; so keep constantly in mind the power house idea, making sure you possess its feeling of strength before attempting to distribute—or combat. There is grave danger here of ill-equipment and defeat for no reason but the world-sapping of your strength of which you have been unconscious. If your weapons fail you, it is because you have allowed this. Distribution is so easy and comfortable when you feel sure of the storage capacity.

So watch out for these two points: the minimizing of your sensitiveness, your susceptibility to adverse influences; and your work on maintaining your force by keeping it in conscious association with the power house. Practice these at your leisure, so that in moments of crisis the clash of action will bring automatic functioning. Make, in this way, a stockade for yourself. Then in times of siege arm yourself with your two points of protection: withdraw from your own sensibilities; work courageously with the associated power.

Betty: If you do these things, combat actually be-

257

comes more or less comfortable and enjoyable! It takes on a kind of Irish quality—any fight better than no fight at all.

Invisible: One more thing in this connection: psychic *dissipation* is not the only ill to which beginners are subject. There are also those who languish from psychic *anemia*. These are the ones who, through an incomplete apprehension of service, seek strenuously to give before they possess. This desire for service, excellent in itself, unless it is kept strong from its source must inevitably bankrupt itself through unrecognized vanity. Thus impoverished, it necessarily loses the authority of amplitude.

Betty: You have to watch this so carefully at first! I am realizing this acutely just now, because at present I am working under the greatest difficulty I have ever had. You see, I used to be like a reservoir that was filled to overflowing, but with no sluice gates for regulation. Consequently I just overflowed automatically, without control, and a lot went to waste. Now I am no longer helped to a superabundance, but have to make my own current by opening definite outlets. As a result, what used to be a great outpouring is now only a thin trickle.

Invisible: Do not be deceived. This thin trickle is worthy of your best attention—even though it does not equal the feel of the current which you first received and sent on its way. That, of course, was a supremely pleasurable sensation: an experience of life itself, the fundamental creative power. But it was not something you could expect to maintain in full force. On setting forth with it, you must anticipate finding it checked, encountering many diffusements. Naturally, this is discouraging. There is an artistic pain in forsaking the full reservoir and strong current with which you started. Nevertheless, a trickle that finds its way contains the same particles of life as the full stream. Remember that.

Betty: I have come to the conclusion that my only *real* responsibility is the trickle, even if it only amounts to a damp spot!

Invisible: Be content. Keep replenishing. Keep going. It is yours, however pitiful. Beginnings are always pitiful. But that is your stage in the great progression. There is nothing unusual about it. You are bringing in a substance that is alien to the environment. Be faithful to it, and never allow any depletion. If for long periods it does not augment, what matter? It is there; and in time, with the growth of wisdom, you will find skill for a full flow.

(Pause.)

Betty: That's just about like me: to have a reservoir, and reduce it to a damp spot!

It is one thing to talk in large general terms about Meeting Life with a Smile, and quite another to struggle successfully through the underbrush of trivial human shortcomings. Even our best friends have small annoying habits, physical peculiarities, heretical views. As someone has truly said, we like them in spite of, and not because of. The problem of how to meet these imperfections was one which the Invisibles particularly stressed.

Betty: (After a pause.) They put me just now in the midst of rubbishy, cluttery, dust-bin conditions—like those areas of made-land built up out of old tin cans. In city dump heaps I have often seen that kind overlaid with good earth, and things growing on it.

Now the problem is: how do I accomplish this in conditions of *mental* imperfection?

(Pause.)

They brought me a deposit of new substance akin to the earth overlaying the rubbish, only this is a mental, more creative substance. They say you can always do that when conditions are rubbishy—even when they seem quite hopeless. And if you persist in it, you can't help winning out....

You see, one of the most fundamental things about all the obstructive refuse you have to contend with, is that it has released its relationship with the ultimate source of life, and is cooling off and dying of decomposition. Once you realize and understand this, thoroughly, you will never be tempted to lose hope and give in. For with this engraved on your mind, it is impossible to entertain personal antagonism: you know too well the reason for things being the way they are. And once above personal antagonism, and aware of your own free power of relationship with the source, you find the way cleared for the bringing in of the fresh, healthy, over-laying material.

Invisible: In this connection it might be helpful to set down something on imperfections. The great trouble with novices in the use of spiritual substance is that expanded consciousness tends to set up a reflex of awkwardness in their treatment of half-formed, imperfect things. Their usual procedure is to wrinkle their brows, tense their minds, and grow harsh-mannered demanding perfection.

Now, one of the most important attributes of the skilled worker and true artisan is that he cherishes the character of the materials he works with—even to the point of utilizing a knot-hole for a decoration. Therefore rule one is always to accept your material's limitations and imperfections—especially in human beings. Never waste time on their faults. A fault commented on with coldness, even if the element of irritation is controlled, is but chilled and set and deprived of the

warm, life-giving quality which would make it susceptible to being overcome and transmuted. Your attention on it is of no help. It merely increases the disjunc-
tion of the consciousness you are trying to integrate.

What, then, to do? The best course is always to reduce your aims to their essential simplicity, and then
seek the co-operation of your material, however imperfect. If you do this, you will quickly find there are endless ways of drawing together in the main issue, without throwing all your force into the byways of imperfection. Nor will you find this too difficult to accomplish—provided you keep as your chief aim the determination to proceed with the least friction and the
most skill and sympathy, in the sense of an artist's
sympathy with his work and material.

This is always the best approach, and in the long run
is bound to be the most effective. Observe the lives of
those who have gone farthest and given most. Wisdom,
a type of tender understanding, surmounts all else in
their human relations—even to the point where they
seem to have lost all ability to censure, and have only
the outpouring desire to hearten. By contrast, how disheartening is amateur spirituality!

Again and again the Invisibles returned to this problem of keeping away from imperfections and antagonisms. I will quote one more discourse which seems
peculiarly illuminating.

Betty: I am looking at the simple practice of approaching sympathetically our problems of human relationship. It looks so obvious and easy, and yet I am
having trouble taking definite hold of it.

Invisible: The first point of attack should be the deliberate inspection of egoism in each living creature—
especially in yourself—and coming to terms with it.

261

What you desire, fundamentally is a generous and spontaneous blending with other lives, but there is a toughened ego-membrane which obstructs. This is that part of you which can be wounded, and which is already sadly scarred by contacts with life. It is the first thing with which you must deal—which you must strip off, if you are to free for action the indestructible self that cooperates with universal force.

Betty: It is very interesting to look at an individual's personality that way—to see his inner potency and possibility compared to his surface representation. It makes it possible to ignore the misrepresenting agents of the man—his habits, indulgences, dormancies—and insist on dealing with his possibilities: to regard, not what he gets snarled up trying to *do*, but what he has inside him that he wants to *be*. I must remember that's the way to do with people.

Invisible: The first requisite, if you are to accomplish this, is to develop a humor of the heart in contemplation of the foibles and follies of people—much as one is undisturbed by the pranks of children. Then your outside will be able to joke and appreciate and be as earthly as you want with their peculiarities, leaving your more fundamental movements under the direction of your inner vision.

This may sound simple and easy at first, but it will require your best efforts. It is very hard to be always big enough to overlap peculiarities, to drag forth the enduring element in each—the *perpetual* person—to throw calmly into discard the barnacle parasite part of people that makes the trouble between them.

Betty: In future I'll try to think of it that way—to think of the poor barnacles as coatings which can be stripped off. After all, there's no sense, after I've discarded my own false front, in dealing any more than I have to with the masks of men. I must lay them aside with what I have stripped from myself, and deal as directly as possible. Then these irritating obstructions and cynicisms will not worry me, because I'll know they belong with my own discards. No use in trying to deal with them, for that just turns you back to your own.

Invisible: It is very important to remember this: that all the disagreeable, snagging contacts with imperfect human nature can be comfortably relegated to a common refuse pile. All you have to do is to regard them without criticism, as a wise physician would; forgetting to blame the cause of the disease, and occupying yourself only with keeping from the contamination of it, in order that you may be in a position to call out healing powers. You will then find it quite simple to confront with your own harmony the problem of disharmony.

Betty: Now that's settled! I'm never going to forget that refuse pile for the frailties of human contacts. It's going to be very comfortable to have to throw things on; both those which I strip off myself, and what I strip off others.

Even granted the best intentions and the most skillful approach, we cannot always be successful. In fact, the best causes often suffer the worst reverses. Therefore our attitude toward defeat is most important. It is more than that: it is one of the most significant threads in the fabric of our days.

Invisible: Confidence in the law is faith. Faith is often called upon to survive seeming defeats of the law. When this occurs, always examine, patiently and trustingly, the seeming defeat to find a wider application of law. It is not defeated. Its enduring materials are simply overlaid with impurities. Some people, for instance, get such avidity for this work that they attack pest spots, and are apparently themselves overcome. But only apparently, and by the lower standards.

Failure you must always regard as an inevitable step toward success. It must not be looked on as a faith-destroying monster. If you search carefully, you will find you can always see around it. Sometimes, of course, you must experience grievous disappointments, but the bitterness of these inevitable failures must be washed away as promptly as the sweat of toil. And once you sensibly accept the probable percentage of negatives in your experiments, knowing that the positive does exist, you will not find it difficult to regard your occasional successes as a sufficient reward.

The important thing is always to keep on as a faithful scientist and explorer. Never let go of your ideals, even if they don't work, except to exchange the particular hold you have on them for a better. Nor must you ever give up treating humanity as though every aspiration of your own were also theirs. Reason tells you that all men are at different stages, and one does not concretely expect responses from the undeveloped. Nevertheless the attitude of always calling for the qualities of manhood, even from a child, is an accepted standard of the proper educational relation. If you are to succeed, it must be maintained, always and always, in spite of reverses and in spite of fitful response.

The radiance of the sun on the waves is as bright as ever, in spite of the fisherman's disregard of it. His myopic concern is mostly with his fish lines, but whenever he lets the beauty of the radiance enter into him, then there is greater unity in creation. Therefore remember this well: radiance should not wax and wane in power depending on the earth's recognition. It is the private affair of a surface continually existent whether or not someone sees the sun shining on it.

Repeated application in the face of defeat: that is the formula. Impress on yourself the necessity for *repeated treatment* to overcome recoil. It is the one great danger, because so many fine people become discouraged, embittered, not understanding. You see it everywhere, for all sensitive individuals feel this recoil. They withdraw in despair, and do not always re-enforce themselves to return. Examine always your reactions in withdrawals. They are fraught with great revelation. Why do you withdraw? Generally because you are not strong enough to fight for your side.

Persistence is not too difficult if your anticipations are moderate. So do not start out expecting to be flattered by spectacular results. Just plan to keep going for the satisfaction of occupying your place in the greater scheme. There will always be moments of full realization, the blooming and fruition natural to all life. That also will come to you in its turn. It is not all strain and effort.

One strives for one's ideals. One seeks to overcome opposition, to take possession of one's opponents, to fulfill to the best of one's ability the particular vision entrusted to him. One must recognize that even in one's success one has incorporated the strength of the opposition, as one incorporates an alien substance for strength in reinforced concrete. Or in the case of failure, one has given of one's best to temper or modify others' success, which is perhaps merely temporarily necessary for the greater stability of the whole. In general one does one's part, always conscious that the final results will be reviewed by a higher judgment.

Search out your ambitions and contemplate them. Stand up and reveal yourself for what you are. Thus only is wisdom and self-direction obtainable. What have you to contribute of your distillation of life? What have you the strength to take of its enduring substances? Rally yourself. Utilize your forces. A boundless universe of unimaginable rapture surrounds each one of us, seeking ever closer relationship. The moment is now to face the slowly obtainable ultimate wisdom of divine consciousness.

CHAPTER VIII

COUNTRY BEYOND

This completes the main outline of the teaching given us by the Invisibles. A quantity of material remains untouched in our "records," but it is more in the nature of detail, either practical or cosmological. As such it would here only confuse the main issues, and must be reserved for possible later publication.

In conclusion I think certain explanations are in order. This book has been made possible only through Betty's pioneering work. It is she who has done the really hard and thankless job of breaking trail. We have simply followed along with the pack train, guided by the charts she has provided.

Why, then, have we presented all this from our own, more mundane, point of view? Partly, as already explained, it is because this individual approach and manner of progress is more typical of the great majority than is Betty's rather specialized experience. Her skyscraping, it seems to us, is something special; something not to be attempted by most. But partly it is because we feel that in this manner we can offer valuable testimony as to the accuracy of Betty's charts: do a trifle better than merely exhibit them. Some of the trails herein described we have tramped back and forth so often that we have proved their reality. Up to a certain point in the teachings we can actually accomplish, and with a fair degree of certainty. We know that they work because we have tried them out with success. And that success has given us confidence in Betty's tracing of the route ahead.

By this we do not mean to imply any important personal accomplishment. In our sophomoric beginnings we were inclined to be moderately cocky, but we have long since got over that. Now we can see that we have not even made a start. We have merely, as the darky said, been getting ready to begin to commence. As to real life, beyond prep-school, we are no more qualified to speak than is any other undergraduate.

On the other hand, this doesn't mean that we are dissatisfied to be where we are; or that we are impatient to "get going." It is simply that we have come far enough along the way to realize that, wherever one happens to be, the road immediately ahead stretches level and far. It is only in the blue distance beyond that one traces the loom of the—as yet—inaccessible peaks. It is only in retrospect that one realizes this point, where he stands, itself once looked high and unattainable.

This strange journey of ours toward eternity is not unlike horseback travel across the spaces of Arizona. I will quote what I mean from something written thirty-odd years ago.

"After a time we came to some low hills helmeted with the outcrop of a rock escarpment. Hitherto they had seemed a termination of Mount Graham, but now, when we rode around them, we discovered them to be separated from the range by a good five miles of sloping plain. Later we looked back and would have sworn them part of the Dos Cabesas System, did we not know them to be at least eight miles distant from the rocky rampart. It is always that way in Arizona. Spaces develop of whose existence you had not the slightest intimation....

"The country was pleasantly rolling and covered with grass. Far in a remote distance lay a slender dark line across the plain. This we knew to be mesquite; and once entered, we knew that it too could spread vastly. And then this grassy slope, on which we now rode, would show merely as an insignificant streak of yellow. It is also like that in Arizona. I have ridden in succession through grass land, bush land, flower land, desert. Each in turn seemed entirely to fill the space of the plains between the mountains."*

So here: the phase of awareness through which we are at the moment moving fills to the limits of our visible world, so that its passage shall bring us to our horizon. But it does not, in actuality, fill our cup; and we shall eventually look back on it as "an insignificant streak of yellow."

Do not mistake, however. This is no prospect of discouraging, infinite and barren effort to reach something that will eternally elude. On the contrary every step of the way is interesting and rewarding. We have not, to repeat, got very far; but already we have been rather overpaid. There is small sense in trying to catalogue all the gains and rewards that warrant this belief. Suffice it that any of us feels it would have been a positive catastrophe had we been able by some magic to overleap to this point; for we should then have here arrived so ill

---

* *Arizona Nights.*

268

equipped that we should have groped into further exploration without eyes to see. By its very nature, this expedition of ours is not a straining rush to a distant goal, but a savoring of the way. For without the full savoring *there is no goal!*

One of the most profound and satisfying truths, which is one of the rewards of the way, is that we should always be delighted that we have not reached any important goal, and that there is still so much more to do. How else are we to get our pay? When a job is over, wages cease. Youth leaps eagerly, all too eagerly, at the end it has envisioned. It needs maturity to realize that culmination is a thing to be touched at last with just a little of regret. For after all, however glad we may be of a comfortable camping place toward night, the thrill of morning is in realizing that the trail leads on and on, into more, and still more, country beyond.

I want you to know that it is all here: everything that you will find anywhere is right here in this world. For instance, this moment I have all the joy and expansion and power that comes from being of the superior substance called spirit, but at the same time I am in a shady street of little garden homes, all leafy and lilacs, with shadows and dropping blossoms. It is as ready here as anywhere for the taking....

Now I am over a gently heaving sea, a sea of sparkles and playful lappings—calm, breathing the deep-bosomed life of ocean-knowing folk. It is very beautiful here, but I think I find more big spirit in the mountains. Their tops are in rare pure sunshine, and all the big elements are their playmates—I like the great thunder coifs they wear on their heads. It is easy to find the spirit of things there.

I find it, too, in the heavy-massed light-shifting sands of the desert, with all its imperturbable wisdom and stoic beauty of indifference—an aloof siren of eternity.

CHAPTER IX

I BEAR WITNESS

Four months ago the manuscript of this book was put in final form and sent to the publishers. And so was completed another full turn in the spiral of Betty's work. But not, apparently, the work itself. According to the Invisibles something of this yet remained to be accomplished—something they refused to define, except that it was different from what had gone before.

"Like a blossom," said they.

"A blossom?" Betty asked.

"Something that occurs at the end of effort, as a demonstration to others. It is a natural attribute of your accomplishment. Of course you *could* go on living as you are, but then you couldn't have the demonstration at the top of your endeavor."

270

At the time the true meaning of this escaped me altogether. My interpretation was that Betty was about to begin another spiral of instruction, with the difference they mentioned appearing largely in the treatment. Accordingly, when she was overtaken only two weeks later by a serious and rackingly painful illness, I was convinced that the success of the job demanded her recovery. It seemed to me defeat at this point would mean that everything we had built up through all these years, and that so many people had taken from us and believed, would crumble into disrepute. And so I fought with every means at my command to hold her back from the Great Adventure.

Another strong incentive to battle, of course, was our natural dread of separation. I shall not dwell on this, but it is necessary to touch upon it sufficiently. We had been married for thirty-five years. In that time we had been apart for but three periods of any length: twice during my explorations into unknown parts of Central Africa; and once during my service in the World War. We had met together the adventures of life, and they had been varied: years of pack horse travel in the Rockies and Sierra; the cattle ranges of Arizona before the movies came; fourteen months in Africa; sixteen seasons in Alaska—here, there, and everywhere in the wild and tame corners of the earth. And adventures also among people, and ideas, and for twenty years the pioneering in these strange dim regions of the higher consciousness.

In the course of this last exploration we had finally arrived at the settled conviction that permanent separation is impossible. Nevertheless it is only human to dread the temporary parting: to contemplate such an interim as something dismal to be endured. I feel sure that this was a stronger consideration with me than with her. There is always a difference between any conviction, however profound, which is arrived at by study and inference; and the understanding belief which comes of experiencing directly the thing itself. For years Betty had been running back and forth to the other consciousness as easily and naturally as a cat in and out of a house—remember her various essays at experimental dying—whereas I had stayed on the inside only looking out. That she should face her final transition to this consciousness with serenity, then, was only to be expected. And it was equally inevitable that, in spite of any amount of philosophizing, there remained in the depths of my being, essentially unmodified, the primitive fear of death and separation.

Accordingly, I now realize definitely, Betty's strongest incentive in her fight was myself. This was not clear to me then, or my own attitude might have been different. She could not foresee how I would take her going, and she was reluctant to burn her bridges. For over two months it was just this that held her, in spite of the greatest pain and in face of what must have been almost overwhelming temptation.

"I could go so easily!" she told me, "at any minute. I have to fight against it in the night." She asked me a little wistfully, "If it came about that way, you wouldn't mind too much letting me go, would you?"

And I, in my ignorance, replied emphatically:

"I most certainly would!"

Two months passed and she became weaker and weaker, until finally the physical frame was worn to the point where only her fighting spirit held her. By now she could only whisper a word at a time, gathering strength for each effort. In the evening the doctor came to the house. I took him to see her, but was not myself looking toward her, when I heard him exclaim: "My God! The woman still smiles!"

Then for the first time I allowed myself to entertain a

doubt as to the wisdom of our persistence. What job could there be that was worth such suffering? A little later Betty closed her eyes. We were not sure whether she was conscious or in coma. I went into another room, sat in an easy chair, and "projected" in her direction as strongly as I could these words:

"You are now where you can decide whether or not the job requires you to stay here and endure this. As far as I am concerned, I release you gladly. I will take you by the hand, go with you just as far as I can, and place it in the hand of the one who is waiting."

A minute or so later the doctor came to tell me it was over: that suddenly Betty had spoken up, as clearly and gayly as had always been her habit.

"It's all right," said she. "I've had a talk with my boy. You can take me now."

Now cames the part I almost despair of setting down adequately. But it is the big thing, and I must try. My first momentary reaction was of relief that she need no longer go through such agonies. The next was a faint but growing surprise that the apprehension of death as a dark veil, an impenetrable barrier, a sharp division was whisked away. It became as thin as a mist. Instead of being a big portentous thing, it was really a comparatively unimportant and trivial detail, after all. Then, as the minutes passed, I became literally astounded that all the things I had been dreading, and bracing myself for, simply weren't there. For it was becoming increasingly, most gloriously, evident to me that the only serious threat of death did not exist.

This next is very difficult to convey. Let me see if I can give an inkling.

You know the cozy, intimate feeling of companionship you get sometimes when you are in the same

273

room; perhaps each reading a book; not speaking; not even looking at one another. It is tenuous, an evanescent thing—one that we too often fail to savor and appreciate. Sometimes, in fact, it takes an evening or two of empty solitude to make us realize how substantial and important it really is.

Then, on the other hand, you know how you draw closer by means of things you do together. And still more through talk and such mental interchanges. And most of all, perhaps, in the various physical relationships of love and marriage.

Now when you stop to think of it, all these latter material contacts, right through the whole of life, are at root and in essence aimed at really just one thing: that rare inner feeling of companionship suggested feebly in the sitting-by-the-fire idea. That is what we *really* are groping for in all friendly and loving human relations, hampered by the fact that we are different people more or less muffled from each other by the barriers of encasement in the body.

Well, within a very few minutes that companionship flooded through my whole being from Betty, but in an intensity and purity of which I had previously had no conception. It was the same thing, but a hundred, a thousand times stronger. And I realized that it more than compensated for the little fact that she had stepped across, because it was the thing that all our physical activities together had striven for, but—compared with this—had gained only dimly and in part. Why not? Actually it was doing perfectly what all these other things had only groped for. So what use the other things? and why should I miss them?

Does this sound fantastic? Maybe; but it is as real and solid as the chair I am sitting on. So much so that I have never in my life been so filled with pure happiness. No despair; no devastation; just a deeper happiness than I have experienced with her ever before, save in the brief moments when everything harmonized in fulfillment.

And furthermore it has lasted, and is with me always.

This, I now believe, is the "great blossom" of which the Invisibles spoke; the final significance to which all of Betty's twenty years of work was to lead. Here is her concrete proof of one reward that can come to those who follow in her footsteps, her final evidence that her instrument of twenty years' forging is strong enough to withstand the supreme test.

Of course I do not delude myself that those who pursue Betty's teachings to this culmination are going to be able, all of them, to gain this point of view in face of loss. Not all of them, nor completely. But it is a demonstration that it can be done; and it is forerunner of what will, one day, be the universal experience of those who follow the trail she has blazed across the unknown.

The End

OTHER BOOKS BY STEWART EDWARD WHITE

In addition to *Across the Unknown*, plans are currently underway to reprint two other Stewart White classics—*The Betty Book* and *The Unobstructed Universe*.

The Betty Book was the first book written by White chronicling the mediumship of his wife Betty and their explorations of the inner dimensions of life. It explains how Betty first discovered her mediumship and how she developed and refined it, as well as setting forth the basic philosophy of "the Invisibles." It should be published by September 1987 in the same format as this book.

The Unobstructed Universe tells the story of the White's ongoing investigations into the inner worlds *after* Betty died. It picks up the story of their adventures where *Across the Unknown* leaves off, with Betty speaking as one of the Invisibles through her good friend Joan, who with her husband Darby had written *Our Unseen Guest*. The result is one of the most brilliant explorations of the fourth dimension ever written. It is due to be published by April 1988.

Like *Across the Unknown*, these two other books by Stewart White will cost $7.95 (plus $1 for shipping). All three books may be ordered by subscription, however, for the low combined price of $21. They will be shipped to subscribers as they are published.

These books may be purchased in leading bookstores throughout the country, or directly from the publisher. When ordering from Ariel Press, be sure to send a check or money order for the full amount of the purchase (plus shipping), or call toll free and charge the purchase to MasterCard or VISA. The toll free numbers are 1-800-336-7769 anywhere in the U.S. except Ohio; 1-800-336-7768 in Ohio.

OTHER BOOKS PUBLISHED BY ARIEL PRESS:

Active Meditation: The Western Tradition
by Robert R. Leichtman, M.D. & Carl Japikse, $24.50

Forces of the Zodiac: Companions of the Soul
by Robert R. Leichtman, M.D. & Carl Japikse, $21.50

Stewart White Returns
by Robert R. Leichtman, M.D., $3.50

Practical Mysticism
by Evelyn Underhill, $5.95

The Gift of Healing
by Ambrose & Olga Worrall, $6.95

Winged Pharaoh
by Joan Grant, $7.95

Far Memory
by Joan Grant, $7.95

Life as Carola
by Joan Grant, $7.95

The Art of Living (five volumes)
by Robert R. Leichtman, M.D. & Carl Japikse, $35

The Life of Spirit
by Robert R. Leichtman, M.D. & Carl Japikse, $7.95

The Hour Glass
by Carl Japikse, $14.95

Edgar Cayce Returns
by Robert R. Leichtman, M.D., $3.50

Nikola Tesla Returns
by Robert R. Leichtman, M.D., $3.50

The Destiny of America
by Robert R. Leichtman, M.D., $7.95

See page 276 for information on ordering.